Kriya Yoga

Kriya Yoga

Sri Sailendra Bejoy Dasgupta

Yoga Niketan

www.yoganiketan.net

email: yoganiketan@yoganiketan.net

surface mail contact:

Yoga Niketan
167 Swakeleys Road
Ickenham
Middlesex
London
UB10 8DN
United Kingdom

iUniverse, Inc.
New York Bloomington

Kriya Yoga

iUniverse books may be ordered through booksellers or by contacting:

iUniverse
1663 Liberty Drive
Bloomington, IN 47403
www.iuniverse.com
1-800-Authors (1-800-288-4677)

ISBN-13: 978-0-595-40347-9 (pbk)
ISBN-13: 978-0-595-67794-8 (cloth)
ISBN-13: 978-0-595-84722-8 (ebk)

Printed in the United States of America

iUniverse rev. date: 7/16/2009

Contents

of Manas from Prana. Resting the involuntary nerves. Pranayama. Preserve of ascetics opened to worldly men. Cleansing Process—Jada Shuddhi, Nadi Shuddhi and Bhuta Shuddhi. Different steps of Kriya. Equivalent of Daiva Yuga, of Kalpa. Higher Kriyas. Realisation of stages of Samadhi and the Pancha Tattvas. Paravastha of Kriya And Paravastha of Paravastha.

[Note: This is the 2006 dedication to Sri Dasguptaji, from Yoga Niketan.]

Introduction

It was the greatest honor of my life to sit at the feet of Acharya Sri Sailendra Bejoy Dasgupta as his disciple in Kriya. An exalted direct disciple of Swami Sriyukteshvar Giri, his spiritual stature was lofty like the mighty Himalayas, yet, while steeped in the highest ecstasies of Kriya, he chose to live quietly, shunning any fanfare or glory. True to the tradition of the greatest Masters of all time he viewed himself as the servant of all.

What is Kriya Yoga? The system taught by Yogiraj Shyama Charan Lahiri Mahasaya and down through his authorized channels is commonly termed Kriya. This book is a rare gem. Written and originally appearing at the end of the author's illustrious life, it is one of the few books available today in which the accurate information on Kriya Yoga is given, historical and otherwise, and written by a man who was part of that sacred tradition during its very crucial years and who had personally known several of the authorized disciples of the Yogiraj Shyama Charan Lahiri Mahasaya (including of course his own beloved Master, the illustrious Swamiji Maharaj, Sriyukteshvar Giri, by whom he was initiated in year 1929 at age nineteen and with whom he remained in close association).

This book is a great rarity in today's world. Nowadays it can be seen that although the system of Kriya has spread and become famous, many of the details and subtleties which were historically part of the system and passed on with great care between Master and disciple have been lost in present times and it is noticed that the science has sometimes been taken out of its original context. The world is full of ever emerging marketers and others making extravagant and irreverent claims, even such fantastic things as claims of personal discipleship/initiations with the Holy of Holies, the secret Mahamuni Babaji Maharaj (Guru of Yogiraj Sri Sri Shyamacharan Lahiri Mahasaya) or other Divine beings in the hopes of deluding gullible people. Poor souls! Therefore the value of this historic book which puts things into correct perspective cannot be understated.

The revered author had received many requests for several decades from such lofty notables as Swami Satyananda Giriji Maharaj requesting him to write such a book but the author refused until the end of his life. At that time, in year 1978 the task was undertaken. As the great man himself wrote—

"at the fag end of his life the author has undertaken what was always considered an impossible task. How the interested readers will react is now out of consideration."

It was his wish that this book "Kriya Yoga" should be presented under auspices of Yoga Niketan and made available to all on a strict no profit basis. I wish to thank the dedicated Kriyavans who worked so hard to make this work possible. By doing so they have served my Master better than I ever could. I bow to the lotus feet of my Master, Acharya Sri Sailendra Bejoy Dasguptaji and to the lotus feet of all the performers of Kriya from all the different lines and traditions all over the world.

In the Omkar,

n.w. "kashi" ("bala gopee")
Yoga Niketan
Portland, Maine
April 2006

1

Preface

Kriya Yoga is an esoteric doctrine of spiritual efforts practised in India from hoary ages by aspirants after Self Realisation and Emancipation from worldly bondage. It is a set of physical and mental techniques by following which consummation of Yoga can be achieved.

In the very first text of the Sadhan Pad (the Chapter on Procedure) of the Yoga Sutras of Patanjali Kriya Yoga has been defined as:

> "Penance (Patience) Studying the Shastras (Vedas and the scriptures) and Divine Contemplation."*
>
> *Tapah Svadhyāhyā Isvara Pranidhānāni Kriyā Yogah. (Sadhan Pad 1)

Patanjali does not only lay down the theoretical definition but emphasises, subsequently in the same chapter, the necessity for cultivating the items that have been shown as constituting Kriya Yoga after inculcation of purity (Saucha) and Contentment (Santosha). It prescribes:

> "Purity (Cleanliness), Contentment, Patience, Studying of Shastras and Divine Contemplation constitute Niyama."**
>
> **Saucha Santosa Tapah Svadhyahya Isvara Pranidhanani Niyama. (Sadhan Pad 32)

Votaries of Tantrik Sadhana and various schools of Yoga also call their technique of Sadhana as 'Kriya'.

But it is the precepts and practices as handed down by Yogiraj Shri Shri Shyama Charan Lahiri Mahasaya that particularly go by the name of 'Kriya'.

Yoga

What exactly does Kriya Yoga signify? The two components of the word—
'Kriya' and 'Yoga'—carry specific meanings. Taking the second component
first, one is immediately reminded of the second text of the first chapter of
the Yoga Sutras, which reads:

> "Yoga is stoppage of attributes of the heart."*
>
> *Yogaschittavritti Nirodhah. (Samadhi Pad, 2)

The above definition of Yoga is in conformity with the formulations of the
scheme of creation as laid down in Samkhya philosophy. Yoga has been
acclaimed as one of the most potent paths adopted from time immemorial
by Moksha Dharmis, the seekers of complete emancipation from worldly
bondages. It has been variously described in the scriptures and Yoga treatises.
Efficacy and powers of Yoga have never been questioned in the long history
of spiritual quests in India. Although to the average man and woman Yoga
may mean esoteric physical and mental efforts which only a hardened
penance-performing recluse can effectively perform, to the initiate Yoga
appears as the only process adopting which one can get over the disturbing
factors, physical as well as mental, in attaining the quietude deemed essential
for Self Realisation. It is no wonder, therefore, fascinating to note that in
almost all the Hindu scriptures and religious literatures one can find essences
of Yoga and Yoga doctrines dexterously woven into the subjects of their
teachings. The great epic Mahabharata and the Shrimad Bhagavad Gita are
outstanding examples in this regard. The Gita is a declared Yoga Shastra, the
Yoga-Shastra-Upanishad, whatever else one may read into its extensive and
priceless message.

In the Gita Yoga has been defined differently under different contexts; each
one of its eighteen chapters has been given a Yoga name. Thus we have Arjuna
Vishada Yoga, Samkhya Yoga, Karma Yoga, Jnana Yoga, Sannyasa Yoga,
Dhyana Yoga and so on. The different names may also indicate different forms
of approach for attaining "Stoppage of Attributes of Heart"—attainment of
Yoga. In modern times one may hear also new Yoga names, for evidently the
same reason, such as 'Integral Yoga,' 'Transcendental Yoga' and 'Kundalini
Yoga.'

Because of the proclaimed efficacy of Yoga practices on the body and mind
of men great interest is evinced even in Western countries for Yoga. It is no
surprise therefore that a large number of Yoga centres have been started in
various world cities. However, what is taught in the name of Yoga in these

centres, or rather what can possibly be taught, is not Yoga proper as known amongst Yoga adherents; but Yogasanas. 'Asana' which is but a seating posture for performing Pranayama was developed by Yogis of yore into a system of physical exercise for maintenance and upkeep of better health. The Asana pertaining to Yoga is one of the steps in the prescribed eight-fold steps of Yoga performances, the Ashtanga Yoga. The eight steps are Yama or the set of don'ts, Niyama or the set of do's; Asana—the seating posture that enables the performer to sit steady and in comfort, Pranayam or controlling of the out-going and in-coming breaths, Pratyahara or reversing of the direction of the senses towards the sensorium, Dharana or evolvement of 'memory', Dhayna or continuing to hold on to the memory, Smriti, and Samadhi or complete concentration.

The common meaning of the word Yoga is 'Union' or 'Link'; it is in this sense that the word has been used frequently in the Gita under different contexts. Methods adopted and paths followed to achieve this 'Union' or 'Link' are also often spoken of as Yoga. This explains the various Yoga names found in the Gita and elsewhere.

'Kriya'

The ordinary meaning of the component 'Kriya' is 'work'. However, in the perspective of spiritual efforts or Yogic Sadhana, Kriya, represents a specially designed mode of efforts, physical as well as mental, which is the secret technique of the Yogis. As mentioned above the Yoga technique handed down by Yogiraj Shyama Charan is known and referred to as Kriya. The technique has passed on from the preceptor to the disciple under rules laid down by the Yogiraj himself for the purpose. Shyama Charan did not himself design the technique of Kriya; he had received it from his Guru, the God-man holy Babaji Maharaj, under mysterious circumstances. It was also never the claim that the holy Babaji Maharaj had himself designed the technique; he also had received it from his preceptor. But that was many hundred years ago, as it is claimed that the Babaji was several hundred years old when he had initiated Shyama Charan into Kriya Yoga. Before Shyama Charan came into the picture Kriya Yoga was a close preserve of the ascetics and hardened Sadhus who lived away from human concourse. The basic ingredients of the technique of Kriya Yoga, however, could be unearthed from the teachings of the Gita, although the actual technique was restricted to a rare number of ascetics. Shyama Charan, and more precisely through Shyama Charan, this monopoly of the ascetics and dwellers of forests and hills had been broken.

Unlike contemporary saints Shyama Charan was a full fledged householder, Grihasta, all through his life. He was already a married man and was holding a Government job when the Babaji Maharaj had 'drawn him' to him and initiated him; subsequently also when Shyama Charan had flowered into one of the most famous saints in Northern India he continued to be a family man and a householder. He begot children, brought them up, gave them proper education and helped them in settling themselves in life. He performed all the tasks of a perfect Grihasta while remaining completely engrossed in the ecstasies of his enlightenment and resigning completely to the Divine. He completed the stipulated years of service with the Government like all other ordinary employees and retired in due course with a pension. But beneath all the appearances he developed himself into one of the most illustrious Yogis of the age. What the famous saint Mahatma Tailanga Swami, the moving Vishvanath of Sri Rama Krishna, had remarked about Shyama Charan at this time would be excitingly relevant.

One day Shyama Charan went to pay respects to the Mahatma; he was clad in the attire of a middle class Bengali gentleman—a house-holder. As soon as Mahatma Tailanga Swami saw him he stood up in joy and as Shyama Charan came near he embraced him. The two were together for some time and then Shyama Charan left. A devotee of the Mahatma who had witnessed this meeting and exchange of greetings then approached the Mahatma and asked, "Maharaj! you are a dedicated Sannyasi, and the person who came to you was but a Grihastha; why then did you show him so much respect?" The great Mahatma replied, "He has attained the Yoga stage, by remaining a Grihastha, to attain which I had to discard even my loin cloth; should I not show him respects?" The above statement of the illustrious Mahatma Tailanga Swami, apart from being an expression of saint-like humility speaks eloquently of the high attainments of Shyama Charan, the rarest Grihasta, in the realms of Yoga Sadhana. How he led his life, seemingly as a confirmed house-holder but inwardly the most consummate Yogi, can be seen from another example.

Shyama Charan was required to make daily purchases from the market of articles of daily consumption. His dutiful wife used to give him the marketing bag and requisite cash. She used to spell out what had to be purchased. Many of the items were common every day and hence did not need repetition. He walked towards the market with the bag in hand and the cash. As soon as he came near the market a flower-vendor came rushing to him, took the bag and the money from Shyama Charan and himself went inside the market. He would make all purchases, as he could easily make out what was needed in such a pious family. He would not forget even the tobacco and lime for the good old lady. Coming back to Shyama Charan, who waited by the road side all this time, the vendor handed over the bag full of purchased articles. Shyama Charan carried the bag home with the merchandise. The good lady thought within herself after inspecting the purchases how lucky she was to have such a considerate and frugal husband. The vendor was seized with inexplicable veneration for Shyama Charan from the very day he saw him; and from that very day he acted as above. Shyama Charan became a totally dedicated tool in the hands of his God and remained totally resigned in all situations of day to day life.

The above picture just offers a glimpse into the very high spiritual state Shyama Charan maintained all the time. A house-holder or a monk made no difference in him. The propounder of Kriya Yoga in modern times was all the time immersed in the sublimities of Kriya Yoga; and all his disciples, whether a monk or a lay man; considered him as the very God in flesh and blood.

Shyama Charan received Kriya yoga from the holy Babaji in 1861 and he breathed his last in 1895. In this span of about thirty four years he had initiated scores and scores of men and women of all caste and creed in Kriya Yoga, many of whom had themselves blossomed into celebrated Yogi saints. Mention may be made in this connection of Swami Sri Yukteshvar, Swami Kevalanada Paramhansa, Paramhansa Swami Pranavananda, Paramhansa Keshavananda, Acharya Panchanan Battacharya, Acharya Braja Lal Adhikary, Acharya Ram Dayal Majumder and Acharya Bhupendra Nath Sanyal who were all his successful disciples. They not only carried on the sacred task of lighting up the flame of Kriya among spiritually thirsty souls of subsequent generation, but through numerous publications on the subject of Hindu Spiritual culture and establishing various Socio-Religious institutions helped in bringing the message of Kriya Yoga to the reach of all.

It will be evident from the above that Yogiraj Shyama Charan made no distinction between a Sannyasi and a Grihastha as long as both were engaged in Kriya Yoga. A person initiated into Kriya, a Kriyavan, was considered by him as equivalent to a twice-born, a Dvija, irrespective of his social and caste standing.

Amongst the several disciples of Lahiri Mahasaya, who left behind rich literatures on Kriya Yoga in particular and Hindu spiritual aspiration in general, names of Acharya Panchanan Bhattacharya, Paramhansa Pranavananda, Acharya Ram Dayal Majumder, Acharya Bhupendra Nath Sanyal and of Swami Sri Yukteshvar appear in bold relief. The most outstanding contribution, however, was that of Swami Sri Yukteshvar. He was the spiritual guide of Paramhansa Yogananda; he quietly built him up for eventually undertaking the magnificent task of carrying the message of Kriya Yoga to America.

When the course of progress of Kriya Yoga is considered in its broad perspective three events spread over about half a century, precipitate in one's mind as three prominent and concrete milestones. And behind each event the holy hand of the Babaji Maharaj is discernible. That the entire course has proceeded in accordance with the design of the mysterious Babaji Maharaj cannot escape one's scrutiny.

The first event was Shyama Charan's meeting the Babaji in 1861 at Ranikhet—a meeting brought about by the wishes and through an exhibition of Yogic powers of the Babaji himself. Shyama Charan's office had mistakenly named him to proceed to Ranikhet in connection with some construction work there for building a cantonment. Shyama Charan went there, met the Babaji who was his Guru even in his proceeding birth, received his initiation in Kriya Yoga, obtained the Guru's permission to spread Kriya to the deserving and desiring souls of the world, and then came to know that his transfer was a mistake. Coming back he engaged himself deeply in the performance of Kriya. He initiated countless men and women of all sects, creeds and climes into Kriya; and the event heralded the breaking of the 'barrier', that kept the secrets of Kriya Yoga confined to hardened ascetics, and out of reach of the ordinary people of the world.

The second event took place in 1894, one year prior to Shyama Charan's passing away from the earthly scene. It took place at Allahabad where a Kumbha Mela was being celebrated. This time it was a surprising meeting between the holy Babaji Maharaj and a disciple of Shyama Charan, Swami Sri Yukteshvar Giri. Sri Yukteshvar at that time had not become a Sannyasi and was still bearing the name given by his parents, Priya Nath Karar. He was at that time a widower and had his only child—a daughter—and the widow mother as dependent members in the family. In this meeting the holy Babaji had inspired Priya Nath to write a book bringing about the similarities between the basic teachings of the Hindu Scriptures and philosophies and the basic conceptions that could be found in the teachings of Jesus Christ in the Holy Bible. The purpose was, as could be gathered after the task had been accomplished, to make the message of Kriya Yoga appear as not so alien and as such acceptable to the Christian West.

The 'apparently accidental' meeting between Swami Sri Yukteshvar and Paramhansa Yogananda, then Mukunda Lal Ghosh, at Varanashi in 1913 constituted the third event. Mukunda Lal was the second son of Bhagavati Charan Ghosh, a senior government servant. Bhagavati Charan and his wife were Kriya Yoga disciples of Lahiri Mahasaya. From his very childhood Mukunda Lal was unusually attracted to Sadhus ascetics. One could easily guess from his attitudes even in that early age that one day this boy would renounce worldly life and become a Sannyasi. He ran away from home after doing his Intermediate Examination in colleges and went to Varanashi in search of a spiritual Guru. It was then and in that holy city that he met Sri Yukteshvar, his destined spiritual preceptor. Perhaps in his deep spiritual wisdom Sri Yukteshvar had seen in this young man the fulfillment of the undeclared wishes of the God-man Babaji Maharaj!

Swami Sri Yukteshvar was born in 1855 in Serampore, a suburb of the metropolitan city of Calcutta. He was the only child of his parents. The parents gave his name as Priya Nath Karar. He had his education in a modern English School; and after having duly passed the Entrance Examination of the Calcutta University got admitted in a College for higher studies. But his studies in the College had been cut off for reasons paradoxically, as a result of his intense desire to learn whatever was taught thoroughly and to his satisfaction. However, Priya Nath was married in due course. His father died soon after, and the wife too died after giving birth to a female child. The burden of looking after the family fell on his unaccustomed shoulders, although his dependent family-members were limited to his widow mother and his baby child. He was not required to earn for the maintenance of the family; whatever had been bequeathed by his father was sufficient to carry them through comfortably.

In 1883 Priya Nath came in touch with Sri Sri Shyama Charan Lahiri Mahasaya and was initiated to Kriya Yoga by the great Yoga Guru. Endowed with all the physical features and mental characteristics of a competent Yogi Priya Nath's progress in Kriya Yoga had been meteoric. He not only mastered the system before the end of the decade but was permitted by Lahiri Mahasaya to become a Kriya Yoga Guru himself. Moreover, with the inspiration and blessings of his Guru Priya Nath started to write systematically Spiritual Interpretations of the Gita.

Serampore was a centre of celebrated foreign Christian missionaries, who by their social service and compassion for the people of the neighbourhood had earned gratitude, respect and affection of the people. As a native of Serampore it was natural that he would come in close contact with them and develop friendship with some of them. As a result of these contacts he became well conversant with the Holy Bible containing teachings of Jesus Christ, and with life and mode of living of Christian evangelists.

The episode of abrupt end of Priya Nath's College education, referred to above, may be of interest, as this would give an insight into the mental make up of the man destined to be a famous religious and spiritual leader that he became in after life. One day he was listening to a lecture in a class on Physics. The teacher was explaining the functions of the human eye and comparing it with the functions of a simple photographic camera. He explained that rays of external objects after passing through the lens of the eye formed real inverted images on the retina, and that the same were seen by the individual as erect due to 'visual impression'. Priya Nath could not appreciate how the inverted image formed on the retina could be seen erect. He stood up and asked the teacher, who repeated what he had said earlier. But this could not satisfy Priya Nath's curiosity; he repeated his question at which the teacher became irritated and remarked that if his explanations were not understood it was as well that the alumni left his class. A very serious young man as Priya Nath was, such rude and unwarranted remark of the teacher was sufficient provocation for leaving the class. He not only left the teachers class but he left as well the College for good. This, however, did not mean that all the doors of knowledge in modern science had been blocked against him. He approached the Principal of the Calcutta Medical College and by persistent requests persuaded him to give him permission to attend classes on scientific subjects such as Physics, Chemistry, Biology, Physiology, Anatomy and the like in that College. He was not preparing to become a physician; hence there was no question of appearing for examinations or following the curriculum of the medical college. He attended the classes to acquire knowledge; sometimes he attended classes on the same subject more than once, when he felt he needed to understand a point clearly and thoroughly. He attended various classes in the Medical College for about two years and acquired fair knowledge on the aforementioned subjects.

Priya Nath was a born mathematician. He always scored full marks in the subject in the school as well as in college. As a consequence he found a natural attraction for Astronomy and Astrology. In course of time he became very proficient in Astrology and, in later life, he became famous among who knew him as a very good Astrologer.

In 1894, hardly eleven years after he had been admitted into the fraternity of the Kriya Yogis, and when he had already become a Kriya Yoga Guru Priya Nath went to Allahabad to witness Kumbha Mela that was being celebrated there that year at the Sangam, the tri-junction of the Ganga, Jumna and the subterranean Sarasvati. He had no desire to go there as a pilgrim to earn religious virtues but to satisfy his curiosity. As a successful Yogi, outward religiosity had no attraction for him. The spectacle of the huge concourse of men and women, laymen and monks and Sadhus, and people representing and belonging to all religious sects and denominations with their distinguishing marks and insignia, including the Nagas—the nude ascetics—was an unforgettable experience for him. He, however, felt there might be many people in America and other Western countries who might not be leading ascetic lives like the hordes of ascetics that had assembled at the Kumbha, but living like ordinary householders who might possess no less spiritual potentialities than many of the ascetics at the Kumbha; some of them might even be richer in this wealth.

One afternoon during the period of the visit Priya Nath crossed the Jumna in a boat from the side of Allahabad to the bank opposite. This side of the river Jumna was known as Jhusi. He crossed over there in order to avoid huge crowds on the Allahabad side. On the Jhusi side also Sadhus and religious men had pitched up tents on either side of the road running along the bank of the river. But this side was not as crowded as the side opposite. Priya Nath was dressed in the attire of a middle class respectable Bengali gentleman; he was strolling along the road and was engrossed in his earlier musings over spiritual potentials of individuals which had no relation to any type of life one might live. He was also thinking about teachings of Christ, some of which appeared to him to be similar to basic conceptions of the Hindus. About this time a monk called him from his back addressing him as Swamiji Maharaj and led him into a tent close by.

As soon as Priya Nath entered the tent he heard a welcoming voice announcing, "Swamiji Maharaj! Take your seat." He saw a very bright and pleasant looking saint smilingly signaling him to take his seat. Priya Nath bowed before the saint in reverence, took his seat sad then said, "Your holiness! I am not a Sannyasi; why then are you addressing me as Swamiji Maharaj?" At this the strange Saint went into a loud laughter and remarked, "It has come out of my mouth that you are Swamiji Maharaj; hence you are surely a Swamiji Maharaj!" Saying this the saint went into laughter again. This unusual reaction surprised Priya Nath and he stopped protesting any further. Priya Nath was impressed by the bright appearance of the strange saint who seemed to him to be a Yogi of a very high order. His pleasant and affectionate behaviour made him discuss with him some of the questions that were agitating him. Taking up the thread of his erstwhile musings he openly gave expression to his impressions that there might be many persons in America and other Western countries who might possess similar spiritual wealth as the ascetics that had congregated the Kumbha, if not more than many. The saint who was listening with interest smilingly nodded approval as Priya Nath had said this. Priya Nath then raised his other favourite theme, that of similarity between Hindu basic spiritual conceptions and basic conceptions underlying some teachings of Jesus Christ. This time also the saint nodding approval remarked, "You have rightly said." Then suddenly the saint proposed, "You have been writing the Gita at your Guru's behest; why not write a book on the subjects you have discussed here, at my behest?" Priya Nath was startled at such an unexpected development and replied in consternation, "What a suggestion Sir! I am not a man of erudition in the Shastras; how can I venture to undertake such a serious task?" The saint, at this, burst into loud laughter in the same way as when Priya Nath protested after having been addressed as Swamiji Maharaj, and remarked, "No one refuses to do my biddings! It has come out of mouth and I also know that this will be accomplished." So saying the saint went into loud laughter again. This devastating laughter washed off Priya Nath's protestations. Calming down Priya Nath pleaded, "Sir, if I am able to write as you have desired shall I see you again?" "Surely" was the reassuring reply of the saint.

From the Kumbha Mela Priya Nath went to Varanashi. There he saw his Guru and narrated to him his experiences at the Mela. He also mentioned about his meeting the strange saint, when he learnt that the saint was none other than the god-man Babaji Maharaj himself, the Guru of his Guru. This was a revelation to him; he realised that the desire expressed by the saint to write the book was not just a passing remark but a veritable divine and holy commandment!

Returning home Priya Nath engaged himself in giving tangible shape to his ideas about the proposed book. To begin with the task seemed an impossibility. However, gradually ideas gathered when he sat with papers and pen, usually at night when everybody went into sleep. Before the end of the year the book was complete. The day the last page was completed it was about day-break and Priya Nath went on his daily routine of bathing in the river Ganga that flowed by Serampore. After having a dip in the river as he started to scale up the steps of the bathing Ghat he was amazed and filled with extreme joy to see Babaji Maharaj beaming with smile standing under a tree on the bank of the river near the Ghat. Priya Nath paced up the stairs of the bathing Ghat quickly and bowed before the great saint in obeisance; he expressed his boundless joy in being able to see him again and requested him to kindly come to his house which was very near. The saint replied that he loved to stay under the tree as he belonged to a class that lived under the trees. At this Priya Nath fervently prayed that the saint might kindly wait a while; he would quickly go home and come back with some milk and fruits. So saying he almost ran home and soon returned with a bowl of milk and some bananas. But where was Babaji Maharaj? He could not find a trace of the god-man in spite of intense search throughout the township. When he returned home tired and frustrated after a couple of hours and entered his bed room his eyes fell on the scattered manuscripts lying on the bed. He at once remembered the assurance given by the very kind Babaji Maharaj that he would see him when he would complete writing the book. His heart was filled with gratitude, reverence and joy, now that the great saint had kept his words. The book was named 'Kaivalya Darshanam, the Holy Science.'

The Holy Science is a marvelous synthesis of the basic features of Hindu spiritual conceptions with the essential teachings of Lord Jesus as contained in the Bible. The texts in the book are in Sanskrit in the tradition of Hindu Shastras while the explanations and interpretations are in English. This is significant and clearly intended for English readers as an introduction to the English speaking world, the Christian world, of the underlying basic message of the Hindu religion.

Sri Yukteshvar was very proficient in Astrology, it has already been mentioned. In his studies he detected certain mistakes in Hindu calendars mainly about dates of certain special Hindu festivals and on the traditional conceptions on the duration of the Yugas, the Hindu millennia. The Sankrantis related to verifiable earthly and celestial phenomena, he averred. But modern Hindu calendars still gave the dates of these festivals as was determined hundreds of years ago without making any adjustments for changes that had taken place during the long intervening period. On the Yugas he showed by elaborately quoting from the Manu Samhita that duration of the Yugas expressed in numbers of years have been shown unnecessarily long and wrongly estimated. According to his interpretations the world had been passing through Dvapara Yuga at present, having passed through two spells of Kali already. The advent of Dvapara which is a better Yuga had meant that man's intrinsic capacity to grasp finer aspects of things; and as such the message of the fundamental spiritual teachings would find better and still better acceptance in the world.

In the year 1900, when Dvapara Era proper had just started after completing its period of mutation of 200 years in the reverse order, Sri Yukteshvar, still Priya Nath, called his disciples and explained the significance of the change of time; he emphasised that the time ahead was propitious when people generally would be able to comprehend finer and finer aspects of men and materials; and that they should now organise something in keeping with the trends of the change of Yuga. Accordingly in the year 1902 a socio-religious institution was established by the name Sat Sanga Sabha. Although he was still living like a house-holder and was still Priya Nath Karar, he now wrote his name as 'Priya Nath Karar Swami.' This was in deference to the way the Holy Babaji Maharaj had addressed him when they met at the Kumbha in 1894. Many eyebrows were raised when this peculiar and uncustomary way of writing one's name was noticed. But Priya Nath did not care for these; he kept his reasons for the peculiarity to himself.

Through the Sat Sanga Sabha were launched various educational, social and spiritual activities in addition to the Sat-Sanga Sabha branches becoming centres for cultivating Kriya Yoga and deliberations on Yoga Shastras. Through the branches the Karar Swami also preached his own ideas on Yuga and other matters touched earlier. Realising that he would be better able to carry on with his activities if he became a formal monk, he went to Bodh Gaya where he was ordained as a Sannyasi by the then Mohant of the Bodh Gaya monastery, His Holiness Paramhansa Swami Krishna Dayal Giri, and was named Swami Sri Yukteshvar Giri.

In the early years of the second decade of the century, sometime in 1912 or 1913 a miraculous meeting took place between Sri Yukteshvar and a young man then named Mukunda Lal, who became world famous later as Paramhansa Yogananda. Late Bhagavati Charan Ghosh was an important Government servant. Both he and his wife were Kriya Yoga disciples of Shri Shri Lahiri Mahasaya. Mukunda Lal was their second son. When he was a mere baby Lahiri Mahasaya, it is said, while blessing him remarked, "This boy will later become an engine," hinting evidently at the future role of the baby. From his very childhood Mukunda Lal showed great attachment for monks and religious men. He was very fond of his mother who possessed a pair of beautiful eyes; but she died when he was still young. Since then he was more drawn to men of religion and spirituality. It is said that when still a baby an ascetic appeared in their house and prophesied that the child would renounce the world and become a Sannyasi in future. His elder brother took up the self-imposed task of protecting the younger brother from spiritual and religious 'contaminations' by refusing to allow him to run to such men. But what the young lad could not openly do, he accomplished surreptitiously. In spite of his reluctance to sit with his books, his education continued according to schedule. He passed the Matriculation Examination and then the Intermediate, when he decided that he would study no longer. He would go round in search of his destined Guru. So one day quietly he fled home; dressed in saffron cloth like a Brahmachari he arrived at Varanashi. He did not know where to go. Eventually Paramhansa Swami Jnanananda Maharaj, President of Bharat Dharma Mahamandal, offered him an asylum.

One day when 'Brahmachari' Mukunda Lal was passing along a crossing of two roads at Varanashi he saw an impressive ascetic figure approaching the crossing by the other road. He was very much attracted by the saintly and impressive figure; but he walked on. Soon he was out of sight, but he felt as if he was unable to move any further. He turned and walked back towards the crossing in quick pace. He was surprised to find that the saintly figure stood on the spot he had seen him. He quickly ran to him and bowed to him by touching his feet. As he was doing so the saintly person raised him by the arm, embraced him and said, "Thou hast come at last my boy!" The saintly person was Swami Sri Yukteshvar Giri. The Swamiji took Mukunda Lal to his residence and by questioning him learnt that he was the son of his co-disciple Bhagavati Charan Ghosh and that he had fled home to take up life of a regular Sannyasi. Sri Yukteshvar kept Mukunda Lal with him, initiated him into Kriya Yoga and persuaded him to go back home and complete his college education; he was assured that he would be ordained as a Sannyasi after he had become a graduate. He was also told that great and noble tasks awaited him for which he had to get himself properly equipped. Mukunda Lal agreed on condition that his further studies would be from the college at Serampore, to allow him to be nearer his Guru all the time. Sri Yukteshvar managed to obtain Bhagavati Charan's permission in the matter. He duly obtained the BA. degree from the Calcutta University; but he ascribed his success to the miraculous powers of his Guru.

Soon Mukunda Lal persuaded the Guru to make him a Sannyasi. His new name was Swami Yogananda Giri. His great desire having been thus fulfilled Yogananda was imbued with a spirit of undertaking some big and noble work. He went to Japan but he did not stay there more than just a few days. Returning, he organised the Brahmacharya Vidyalaya, in 1917 on the pattern of Ashramas of old, for education of boys and obtained the patronage of Maharaja Sir Manindra Chandra Nundy of Cossimbazar. This unique institution had attracted notice of all noted public men and leaders of society throughout the entire country in course of time. The institution was later permanently established in Ranchi.

In 1920, when Yogananda was in the Ranchi Vidyalaya, one afternoon while inspecting the kitchen stores he had a vision that he was lecturing before a large gathering of American men and women. He immediately announced on the spot that he would go to America. That what he said was just not a pious wish was shown when he was seen packing up to catch the train to Calcutta the same evening. In Calcutta he moved heaven and earth to find an avenue for going to America. To his joy he learnt that a Conference of the Worlds Fellowship of Faiths would be held that in Boston. He succeeded in procuring a delegate membership to that conference; his father at last offered financial assistance when he learnt that the son had failed to obtain any from elsewhere. A berth was booked in a ship that was leaving for America from Calcutta and Yogananda got into the ship on the scheduled day of departure. He forgot all this time to meet his Guru, inform him about the impending departure and seek his advice and guidance. The Guru, however, was not in the dark. He kept information of every step that Yogananda had taken. On the day of his departure, with the ship waiting at the jetty, Swami Sri Yukteshvar appeared on the scene armed with a pass from another disciple who was a stevedore of the Calcutta Port. He scaled up the ladder of the ship and stood at the door of Yogananda's cabin. Yogananda exclaimed out in great joy and fell on the Guru's feet. He was, at same time, smitten by shame and remorse for keeping the Guru in the dark about his sensational move-ments. However, seeing the Guru he was reassured of the Guru's continued concern and affection for him. He was in tears in sheer joy and gratitude. But there was no time to waste; the Swami took the disciple inside the cabin and the two were together for some time. The Guru handed over a copy of the Holy Science to Yogananda advising him that contents of the book should be the basis of his mission to America.

Thus the three significant events that took place in the span of about fifty years cannot be taken as isolated events;—the ones that took place in 1861 at Ranikhet, at Allahabad in 1894 and at Varanashi in 1913. They appear to have happened under an unseen command and mysterious design for propagation and progress of Kriya Yoga—India's hoary Spiritual Culture.

The present treatise is an attempt to offer a critical estimate of the contribution of Swami Sri Yukteshvar, one of the greatest disciples of Lahiri Mahasaya and an important actor in the above grand drama.

The first discussion in this book has been devoted to an estimate of the Spiritual Interpretation of the Shrimad Bhagaved Gita. The Gita forms a part and parcel of the epic Mahabharata, and is considered to encompass all the essential teachings of the Upanishads. In developing the spiritual interpretations Sri Yukteshvar depicted the story of the Mahabharata as an allegorical representation of the postulates of Sankhya and other basic philosophies. By putting the various names of the epical drama to etymological derivation he has shown that they are but formulations as laid down in Sankhya, Patanjal and other philosophies. Hindu epics, he opined, were but Vedic novels depicting essential features of the Vedas in the form of fascinating stories. King Shantanu, he has shown, represents the Param Purusha postulate of the Sankhya, while his queens Ganga and Satyavati represent the Purusha and Prakriti postulates of same philosophy. The eight sons of Shantanu by Ganga are the Ashta Vasus—the eight aspects or notional representations of the Purusha, the Chaitanya or the Spirit, in the different stages of the chain of creation. Of these, seven aspects are beyond comprehension of men and hence considered immersed; the eighth is comprehensible as the 'Witness'—Sakshi—of the created scene. Satyavati is the Prakriti, which is described as but the state of equilibrium the three fundamental qualities or Gunas—the Sattva (Sentient), Raja (mutative or kinetic) and Tama (Static). The deformations (Vikriti) that the Prakriti undergoes under the 'impact' of the presence of Purusha, the Spirit,—the chain of creation—are depicted as progenies of Satyavati—the Prakirti. In the context of the definition of Prakriti as stated above its deformations are but constructions and manifestations of the Gunas in their different proportions. The very first deformation is called the Mahat Tattva which is the first child born of Satyavati, named Chitrangada (that one whose Anga, form, is colored—Chitrita). The name in the Mahabharata thus would appear significant. Similarly the names of other progenies.

The names also of the actors and actresses in the battle of Kurukshetra as found in the Gita have been shown by Sri Yukteshvar as conforming to the different formulations of the Yoga Sutras of Patanjali. The battle of kurukshetra represents the constant inner conflict a person aspiring after self emancipation is confronted with. The position of every being can be described in the context of its various attributes as set in the broader and wider perspective of the universal scene; while the individual 'forms' may be described as the Kurukshetra, the wider collective perspective induced under the spirit provides for the Dharma Kshetra. The guidance offered by the Gita for attaining emancipation is performance of Nishkam Karma—work bereft of desires. That this is very important and at the same time extremely difficult has been emphasised at various stages of the holy book; because it is extremely difficult to know what constitutes such a work. It declares that one should know what is correct Karma, what is Vikarma or specified or wrong Karma and what is Akarma or non-work. The secret, according to the Gita, is to see Karma in Akarma and Akarma in Karma, which would appear as a fallacy! But seen in the light of the Spiritual Interpretations the teaching is found to be the most correct and a potent one. In its third chapter the Gita says that Karma was evolved out of Brahma and Brahma out of the Indestructible—

the Akshara; and that as a consequence Brahma is all-pervasive and present in all basic Karma, Yajna or holy work.*

*"Karma Brahmodbhavam Viddhi Brahma Akshara Samudbhavam Tasmāt Sarvagatam Brahma Nityam Yajne Pratishthitam." (III, 15)

In the eighth chapter Karma has been specifically defined. It says that the Param Brahma is the Indestructible; the 'idea of self' is the Adhyatma and the divine 'nature' of evolving 'ideas of beings' is the Karma.**

**"Aksharam Brahma Paramam Svabhāvo Adhyātmamuchyate Bhutabhāvo Udbhavakara Visarga Karma Samjnitah." (VIII, 8)

In the fourth chapter the principle underlying the sequences of manifestations in the course of the Yugas has been explained by Sri Yukteshvar in a novel but logical manner. This interpretation, as will be found during discussion on the subject in the book, goes counter to the common belief that the Gita has laid down when God 'descends' on the earthly scene for salvation of humanity—for Avatar-hood. According to his interpretation of the theme the creative scheme is a continuous process, a sequence of manifestation and its absence like the sequence of day and night in an unending chain. This chain of sequences or 'appearance' and 'disappearance' is ascribed to the functions of Prakriti; the secret of attaining emancipation is to achieve identification with the underlying Spirit that exists in every form, which is the ultimate cause of creation. In the fourteenth chapter it says that Mahat Brahma, the first manifestation of deformation of Prakriti, is 'my womb' wherein I cast my 'seed' and whence all the beings appear or evolve.*

*"Mama Yoni Mahat Brahma Tasmin Garbham Dadhāmyaham Sambhavo Sarvabhutanam Tato Bhavati Bharata."

All the forms and beings are thus subjected to the unending process of appearance and disappearance, of coming and going, of births and deaths. In the eighth chapter, the secret of how to get out of the clutches of this unending chain has been given as identification with the Self within.**

**A-Brahma Bhuvanāllokha Punarāvartinoh Arjunah Māmupatya Tu Kaunteya Punarjanma Na Vidyate."

All beings from 'Brahma' downwards are subject to the process of coming and going again and again; but reaching Me there is no re-birth.

The Gita by offering superb logical arguments and providing keen analysis from stage to stage constitutes the best guide for attaining such identity with the Spirit which is the Yoga. The Gita, is as such, designated as the 'Upanishad of the Yoga Shastras' (Yoga Shastra Upanishad).

The process of the unending chain of appearance and disappearance in the scheme of creation, mentioned above, has been the subject of discussion in a separate chapter in this book with the title 'The Yuga'. The enunciation and definition as well as description of the different Yugas, as explained by Sri Yukteshvar, will be seen as a departure from the traditional and hitherto accepted norms. The simultaneous circular movements of the earth round its axis, of the moon round the earth, of the earth with its moon round the sun and the Hindu astrological conception of the sun with its family of planets and satellites in relation to the Vishnu Nabhi, the Prime Centre of the Universal process, are all attuned to the Grand Scheme of creation. With quotations from the Manu Smriti it has been shown that the traditional descriptions of the Yugas with fearful lengths of duration are based on erroneous appreciation of what the Shastras on the subject have laid down.

According to Sri Yukteshvar duration of a Yuga no doubt extends over thousands of years, but it is not as long as over hundreds of thousands of years as the traditional almanacs would have us believe. He has also shown that the astronomical phenomenon of 'Precession of Equinox' has got some relation with the advent and passing away of the Yugas, the Satya, Treta, Dvapara and the Kali. A Daiva Yuga is the aggregate of the durations of the above four Yugas. One thousand Daiva Yugas constitute a 'Day' of Brahma, the Creative Force, during which creation remains manifested; while a similar number of Daiva Yugas constitute Brahma's 'Night' when Creative Force goes into its 'slumber' and creation is withdrawn, to re-appear again at the end of that length of time constituting its 'night.' The Satya Yuga commences when Autumnal Equinox occurs at the first point of Aries; as a result of the phenomenon of precession of equinoxes, for the equinox to occur at the same first point of Aries again a period of twenty four thousand years have to elapse, taking the quantum of precession per year as fifty four seconds (54") according to Surya Siddhanta. In this long course two sets of the above four Yugas develop—one in the descending arc from Satya to Kali and the next one in the ascending order in the opposite direction. Sri Yukteshvar has shown by calculation that the earth and the solar system are at present in the ascending arc and are in the Dvapara Yuga, after having passed through the Kali quartet of the ascending arc, and not in the earlier stage of Kali's Sandhya, mutation period, as announced by the traditionalists. The Yugas are associated with developments of certain inner mental virtues, in the general way, and manifestation of such virtues on the general plane is ascribed to the

Yuga effects. But an individual is capable of manifesting these virtues in a very short span of time, within the space of one's own life time, if procedures of the Universal process are enacted within himself. Kriya Yoga has been patterned in line with this Universal Process.

The Holy Science is a master piece in the realm of spiritual literatures laying down the essential base of Kriya Yoga in context of the general concepts of almost all the spiritual literatures of the Hindus, and showing parallelisms with the essential teachings of Christ; teachings of Christ, as he read them, from the different quotations selected from different books of the holy Bible. He picked up several quotations from different books of the Bible which, he has shown, bear surprising similarities to the Hindu spiritual conceptions.

The Holy Science is divided into four chapters. The first chapter is titled the Veda or Gospel. In this chapter concepts of creation found in Samkhya with Param Purusha, the Ananta Chaitanya the Param Brahma has been depicted as the Only Real Substance that exists—the *Sat*—and has been put in as analogous to the God-The-Father of the Christian faith, the Supreme Spirit. Two aspects of the above Supreme Spirit are (i) the Almighty Force, Shakti or '*Ananda*' and (ii) the Omniscient Feeling Love, the *Chit*. These constitute Sat-Chit-Ananda aspects that are at the root of all appearances as well as of all conceivable existences.

The Almighty Force Shakti exercises force which results in a sort of vibration that emanates the celestial sound Pranava, Omkara, which in its wake gives rise to ideas of Time, Space and of Unit. These four items, the Pranava and the ideas of time, space and of unit form the fundamental constituents that provide 'cover' against the Spiritual Light and are collectively called Maya. Units of the above conglomerated collective are the 'Avidyas'. Under the attractive pull of the Omniscient Love, Chit, Maya does not 'receive' these Spiritual Rays but reflects them. However, the divine Attraction of "Chit" brings about changes in the 'Cover' Maya as in the case of a magnetic material, like iron filings, in an electromagnetic field. The resultant end-results have been shown as those in the Sankhya postulates of 'twenty four' principles culminating in the evolution of ingredients of gross matter. These four ideas of sound, time, space and unit have been shown as 'Four Beasts' round the 'throne of the Father' in the Biblical quotation and the twenty four principles as the 'twenty four elders.'

With the manifestation of the above, the Omniscient Love, the Prema Vjja, becomes predominant and under its impact the above ingredients come together forming different stars, planets and satellites and hills, mountains, rivers and plains. The divine 'Prema', Love, continues with its attraction, with the result that gradually plants, living creatures and men evolve. Ultimately the effect of the same Omniscient Love pulls the man out of the veil of Avidya and Maya and leads him into the realms of the Spirit, to the Altar of God the Father and to ultimate identification with Him—which is Kaivalya.

In line with the concepts of the Vedanta different stages of above developments have been shown as divided into seven spheres, Sapta Svargas, and seven nether regions, Sapta Patals—the Fourteen Worlds or Chaturdash Bhuvanas. Of the seven Svargas the fourth which is considered as the sphere of Pranava stands in between the realms of the Spirit—the Jana, Tapa and Satya Lokas and the realms of creation—the Sva, Bhuva and Bhu Lokas. The sphere of Pranava is called Mahar Loka. It has been further argued that while Bhuloka is the sphere of gross matter, Bhuvarloka the sphere of fine matters like electricity and Svarloka is the sphere of very fine matter like magnetism. The Bhuvarloka is also called Sunya and Svarloka as Maha Sunya. Jana Loka has been described as the sphere of 'Christs,' Tapa Loka as the sphere of the Holy Ghost,—the Altar of God the Father, and Satya Loka the stage of the Supreme Spirit—Param Purusha, the God the Father.

In line with Vedantic conceptions again the Jiva or the 'being' has been shown as provided or cast within five sheaths, Panch Kosha,—the Annamaya, the Pranamaya, the Manomaya, the Vijnanamaya and the Anandamaya Koshas. Under the divine attraction of the Omniscient Love the sheaths gradually unfold one by one. Thus with the withdrawal of Annamaya, Pranamaya is revealed with the concomitant appearance of vegetation manifesting life, Prana. Pranamaya withdrawn, Manomaya ushers in revealing appearance of creatures exhibiting rudiments of functions of Manas, the mind. When Manomaya sheath also is withdrawn evolution of man becomes possible who is endowed with 'intelligence,' Buddhi or Vijnana. Vijnana Maya sheath is unfolded only to the highly spiritual saintly souls like Christ who revel in the ecstasies of unceasing joy, the characteristic of the Ananda Maya Kosha. Removal of this last sheath heralds complete emancipation, Kaivalya, merger in the Spirit.

The seven nether worlds, according to Sri Yukteshvar, are to be found within the human body and not 'under ground'. They are the subtle Shat-Chakras experienced by Yogis within the Shushumna and the Sahasrar in the brain, within the Bhu Loka. Counting these seven stages within Bhuloka the Mahar Loka becomes the tenth sphere, with Bhuva and the Sva as the eighth and the ninth. Hence this sphere Mahar Loka is known as the Dasham Dvar, the door between the realms of the Spirit and those of creation.

The second chapter of the book is titled 'Abhishta' or the Goal. It is a small chapter and in the context of what have been stated in the chapter on the Gospel the goal of man has been laid down as attaining Kaivalya, complete emancipation, which is identification with the Supreme Spirit.

The third chapter is called 'Sadhana', Procedure. How to discipline oneself for the above 'goal' has been described in this chapter. Although the very first text reads like the one in a chapter of similar name, 'Sadhan Pad', in the Yoga Sutras, Sri Yukteshvar has described Tapah—patience and penance, Svadhyaya—studies of the Shastras and the Vedas and Brahma Nidhan (instead of Ishvara Pranidhan of the Yoga Sutras) as constituting Yajna or holy work (and not Kriya Yoga as in Patanjal). His subsequent proposition follows this original postulate. The path to Brahma has been shown as the path of Pranava. This is in line not only with his own thesis as laid down in the previous chapters but in line with the teachings of some Upanishads. The procedures advocated is manifestation of Pranava and sustained efforts to remain merged in this holy 'sound'. It is only by continued merging in the Pranava that an aspirant can get over the 'veil' brought about by the very emergence of the sound at the beginning of the creation process.

In common with the Yoga Sutras the last chapter has been designated as Vibhuti or Revelation. The subtle experiences that a Yogi enjoys have been described. The most interesting exposition is the interpretation given to the Yogic powers of Astha Siddhis, which are at times derided by general religious teachers. Sri Yukteshvar described them as 'Ascetic Majesties' which only a master Yogi, who has got over the veil of Maya and has been thus in 'link' with the Universal Force Brahma, can acquire. These are not 'tricks' at least the actual Siddhis. These are like the ones said to have been performed by Vishvamitra of tradition.

A discussion has also been attempted in this book on the technique of Kriya. Kriya has to be obtained direct from the preceptor and hence any intellectual discussion is improper and risky, and also may be harmful. It has, however, been discussed in the barest outline to show that the technique has been designed by incorporating different items from different Yoga Shastras that are considered congenial to the basic principles of Yoga.

The last discussion has been devoted to a resume of what has been discussed in the previous chapters with a view to pin point Sri Yukteshvar's interpretations, and a brief account of how Kriya Yoga has been catered to the people of America and the West.

Advent of Sri Sri Shyama Charan Lahiri Mahasaya and his activities and those of his celebrated disciples have given a new dimension to the spiritual pursuits and bequeathed to the generation to come a marvelous system of Sadhana. Contribution of Sri Yukteshvar in this respect has been unparallel. It has been desired that his teachings should be put before the interested readers throughout the world in their proper perspectives.

The author is fully conscious of his limitations, both intellectual and spiritual. It was due to these factors that persistent requests from friends and well wishers to write about Sri Yukteshvar for the last twenty five years or more could not be accepted; the foremost among whom was Swami Satyananda Giri Maharaj who, alas! is no more. However, at the fag end of his life the author has undertaken what was always considered an impossible task. How the interested readers will react is now out of consideration. With the passing away one by one of all who had the great fortune of sitting at the feet of the great Master, the hapless author may be excused if in his exuberance and incapacity the great teacher has been in any way misinterpreted or if any wrong information given.

21st September, 1978

Barrackpore   Sailendra Bejoy Dasgupta

2

The Gita

F

Spiritual Interpretations

The first work of Swami Sri Yukteshvar was his 'Spiritual Interpretations' of the Gita. Yogic spiritual interpretations of this supreme Hindu scripture was not a new theme; such interpretations had been made in the remote past by celebrated Yogi-scholars. Swami Sri Yukteshvar's specialty was in explaining in cohesive manner the message of the Gita as an exposition of the basic concepts of Yoga. However, these interpretations were not wholly his but basically of his famous and illustrious Guru Sri Sri Shyama Charan Lahiri. Sri Yukteshvar, of course, provided some modernistic explanations. After having been initiated to Kriya in 1883, Sri Yukteshvar used to frequently visit his Guru at Varanashi and to pass long hours in his company. He used to take notes of the discussions and interpretations the great Yogi used to give on the teachings of the Gita and other Hindu scriptures. With the permission of the Guru and with his blessings Sri Yukteshvar started a weekly meeting at his Serampore home where Gita was systematically read, discussed and interpreted. This weekly congregation was called the 'Gita Sabha'. Gradually these weekly sittings became very popular and were well attended and participated by even traditional scholars of the township. Sri Yukteshvar led these meetings and spiritual interpretations were provided by him. Detailed notes of these interpretations were taken, and once a chapter of the holy book was finished the notes were developed into a cohesive article. At his subsequent visit to Varanashi Sri Yukteshvar used to carry this finished article with him and place the same before his Guru for perusal and approval. In this way the first nine chapters of the Gita had been completed; these were published in a book form later.

Sri Yukteshvar contended that the principal teachings of the Gita could be found in the first nine chapters, and that subsequent nine chapters were but elaborations of what had been already laid down in the earlier chapters.

The Gita is a part and parcel of the epic Mahabharata; the eighteen chapters beginning with the twenty fifth of Bhishma Parva constituting the Gita. However, the present day editions of this holy book show a total of seven hundred verses, while according to a verse in the Bhishma Parva the total number of verses should be seven hundred and forty five. The relevant verse reads:

> "Keshava (Krishna) spoke six hundred and twenty verses, Arjun fifty seven, Sanjaya sixty seven and Dhritarashtra one; this is the measure of the Gita".*

> *"Shasatāni Savinsāni SlokānāmPrāha Kesavah Arjuna Saptapanchāsat Saptashashthi Cha Sanjaya Dhritārashtra Slokamekam Gitāyāh Mānamuchyate."

Modern scholars, however, have discovered Gita, in manuscript form, containing a total of seven hundred and forty five verses.

Position of the Gita in the Hindu religious and cultural life and spiritual pursuits is above all other scriptures; equal only to the Upanishadas and the Brahma Sutra. In the Vedanta philosophical concepts these three scriptures—the Gita, Upanishadas and the Brahma Sutra—are referred to as Prasthana Traya—the Trilogy of Reference. For clarification of any point in any of the said three scriptures a Vedantin will refer to either of the other two. These are known as Shruti Prasthan, Smriti Prasthan and Nyaya Prasthan. Upanishadas, being part and parcel of Shruti or the Vedas constitute Shruti Prasthan; the Gita, being part and parcel of Mahabharata which is a Smriti literature, is Smriti Prasthan and Brahma Sutra having been considered as having final authority on vedic logic is Nyaya Prasthan. The Gita has always been considered the epitome of all Hindu scriptures, containing the essences of the Upanishadas. In acclaiming the Gita the following verse is often quoted:

> "All the Upanishadas are (likened unto) cows, son of Gopal (Sri Krishna) the milkman, Partha (Arjun) the calf, the wise enjoy and the potent nectar,—the Gita,—the milk."*

> *"Sarvopanishado Gāvo Dogdhā Gopāla Nandana Pārtha Vattsa Sudhirbhoktā Dugdham Gitāmritam Mahat."

Nil Kantha Suri, an early commentator of the Mahabharata, eulogised the Mahabharata and the Gita as follows:

> "Essence of all the Vedas exist in the Mahabharata, and the essences of the Mahabharata exist in the Gita; Hence the Gita is the epitome of the scriptures."**

**"Bhārate Sarvavedārtha Bhāratarthascha Kritsnasah Gitāyāmasti Teneyam Sarvasāstramayi Gitā."

Swami Sri Yukteshvar held that epics like the Mahabharata were but Vedic novels. In the garb of popular stories strewn with healthy moral and social lessons the epics offered essential Vedic teachings which, however, had to be dug out from the apparent superficial crusts of the stories. Further, scriptures like the Gita and the Mahabharata, he opined, were amenable to three types of interpretations: Adhibhautic, Adhidaivic and Adhyatmic—material, celestial and spiritual. The Adhibhautic picture of the story of Mahabharata is as follows:

In ancient India there was a King named Santanu at Hastinapur who belonged to the famous Solar Dynasty (Surya Vansha). He had two queens named Ganga and Satyavati. Ganga was the first queen, and after she had left him Satyavati was married.

One morning when the King was strolling along the bank of the river Ganga he was struck by the sight of an unusually beautiful lady on the bank of the river. Her charms completely captivated the King and he became very much desirous of marrying her. The King came to the charming damsel and expressed his desire to marry her. The beautiful lady, it must be remembered, was the river Ganga itself anthropomorphised. The lady agreed to the proposal of the King, but on condition that the king must not protest against any work that might be done by her after she became his queen, and that if he did she would forsake him then and there for good. The King was so infatuated that he readily agreed to the conditions without much thought of consequences. The King took Ganga to his palace as his queen and was beside himself in joy. He received the first jolt in his feelings when he saw that immediately his first son was born Ganga wrapped it up in clothes, carried it to the river Ganga and threw into its waters. He was stupefied at this unheard of heartless action of his queen. But remembering the conditions of their marriage he had to keep quiet. After this the queen behaved in the same way with six more sons born to her and drowned all of them in the waters of the Ganga. The King was very mortified but had perforce to keep himself in check.

When the eighth son was born and queen Ganga was going to carry it to the river as in the cases of the earlier seven sons King Santanu could no longer control himself. Coming to Ganga the King implored her to desist from this inhuman, heartless and cruel act. At this Ganga looked at him, handed over the new born child to him and uttered, "You have violated the condition of our wedlock by opposing what I was doing; keep your child; I am leaving you for good." So saying queen Ganga rushed to the river Ganga and plunged herself into the river and vanished. King Santanu was filled with extreme grief and pain, but things developed in such a quick sequence that he could not do anything in the matter. Under the circumstances his only solace was his eighth son, who was the only survivor among the eight sons born of queen Ganga.

Santanu became very fond of his eighth son who had been named Deva Vrata; he poured all his kingly cares and royal affection on the child. In due course Deva Vrata grew up into a very lovable prince, loved not only by the King but by all the subjects of the kingdom. The prince was given training in all branches of princely qualities, and in every branch he became thoroughly proficient. King Santanu was very happy with prince Deva Vrata in every respect.

One day after Deva Vrata grew up into a very competent prince, Santanu went on a hunting expedition to the forest. Prince Deva Vrata was left in the palace. It was about midday when the expedition reached the midst of the dense forest with the sun up in the meridian. The King stood under the shade of a tree on the bank of a river to take some respite from the excessive heat. Soon his eyes caught sight of the spectacle of a chain of lotus flowers flowing along the current of the river. Following the stream of flowers to their source he saw a handsome girl pouring lotus flowers into the river ritualistically by way of worship. The girl looked so beautiful in the background of the sylvan scene that the king was very much charmed; so much so that he was unable to turn his eyes from the charming damsel. He took position behind the trunk of the tree to ensure that the girl did not see him while he was watching her with captive eyes. After a while the girl was seen getting up and moving out. The infatuated King also followed her but from a distance and in the quiet, so that she might not notice him. When she entered home after traversing some distance Santanu came to the door and called out for the house-holder. Dasa Raja, the fisher-king, who was the lord of the house came out; he was surprised at the sight of the King of Hastinapur at his door whom he immediately recognised. With due respects Dasa Raja inquired of the King what service he could render to his majesty. The King stated that he wanted to marry the girl who had gone to the river a little while ago, who he surmised was his daughter. He requested Dasa Raja to give his consent to the proposal. Dasa Raja was overwhelmed with joy inwardly at this unexpected good fortune for his daughter Satyavati, but outwardly he made expressions as if there was nothing to be wondered at that. There was no question of his withholding consent, he replied. He remarked that she would be a member in the Kings palace at Hastinapur which in itself was a great allurement, but she would be just one of the many members in the King's harem. The King immediately replied that his daughter would be made his principal queen. Realising the intense desire of the King to marry his daughter Dasa Raja was highly pleased but he decided to make a little more bargain for the sake of Satyavati. He said that the announcement made by the King was befitting his great dynasty and that he was more than satisfied. However, there was one more question that lurked in his mind about any son that might be born of Satyavati but that was an impossible question. When the most lovable, competent and universally popular prince Deva Vrata was there this point should not have arisen in his mind at all. He was thinking about succession to the throne of Hastinapur after Santanu's death. Hearing this Santanu immediately recoiled. How could he, even in dream, think of any one else other than his very dear son Deva Vrata would ascend the throne after him? He left the place without uttering any more word and hurried back to the palace.

Santanu, however, was not reconciled. He continued to suffer from intense pain at heart for his failure to marry Satyavati. The charm and beauty of Satyavati haunted him all the time. For most of his time he stayed indoors and started to neglect even essential work of his court and his royal duties. The courtiers noticed this change in the King and gradually everybody became aware of the King's mental unhappiness. Reasons for this grief also became known slowly to most of the people that counted. Prince Deva Vrata also noticed his father's unhappy disposition. By close investigation he came to know the cause and immediately resolved to step in to remove all impediments in the way of his father's happiness. Without telling anybody he set out for Dasa Raja alone and met him and persuaded Dasa Raja to agree to the proposal of his father to marry Satyavati. To reassure Dasa Raja about the future prospects of his daughter and the daughter's future son Deva Vreta swore two astounding vows. By one he vowed that he would never claim the throne of Hastinapur in life; and by the second he announced his resolve not to ever marry so that he would not leave behind any progeny who could put any claim to the throne even in futurity. Two very great and epoch-making vows! for which Deva Vrata henceforth became known as Bhishma. Deva Vrata brought Satyavati to the palace and presented her to his father. Santanu was beyond himself in joy and heartily made Satyavati his principal queen. Satyavati bore the King two sons, Chitrangada and Vichitravirya. Chitrangada was short-lived and died young and Vichitravtrya was a weakling of a prince. However, after Santanu's death Vichitravirya was duly made king of Hastinapur but the kingdom was ruled by the prowess and acumen of Bhishma.

When Vichitravirya attained marriageable age Bhishma thought that the king should have a queen. At about this time an announcement had been made that there would be a Svayamvara Sabha at the court of king Kashiraj where his three princesses would choose their husbands. A Svayamvara Sabha was an exclusively princely affair in where appeared kings and princes of different principalities and the princess would personally choose her husband from amongst the assembled. Some times stakes were set to decide the issue of choice as in the case of Sita in Ramayana, Draupadi in the Mahabharata. Rama had to bend the great bow of Mahadeva by lifting the heavy and massive bow staff to fasten string to it. No body dared to try this as it was considered to be an impossible task. Rama not only succeeded but he pulled the string with such force that the heavy bow staff broke. In the case of Draupadi all the kings and princes present failed to shoot an arrow through a moving wheel placed overhead, looking down on water kept below in which fell the image of the moving wheel and a golden fish placed above the wheel, and pierce the fish through the eye. When no royalty succeeded in the attempt it was announced that any one present in the assembly could try his luck even if he was not of royal descent. The five Pandavas who were then passing through their year of incognito were present in the assembly in the guise of Brahmins, and Arjun accepted the challenge and eventually succeeded.

To the Svayamvara assemblage called by Keshiraja Bhishma himself went being conscious of Vichitravirya's general lack of ability and prowess. Bhishma, however, did not enter the hall of the assembly but kept hiding with his chariot at some distance from the place of Svayamvara Sabha. The three princesses came out before the assemblage soon after, with garlands in their hands, looked around and moved on. As soon as they arrived at a vantage point Bhishma rushed in, carried away the three princesses by force on to his chariot and sped away. The assembled kings and princes were taken a-back at this sudden development and were stupefied for a while but soon woke up to the reality. They gave a chase to Bhishma but were no match for the unexcelled dexterity and power of arms of Bhishma, who successfully made his way for Hastinapur.

Attempting to forcibly carry away Svayamvara brides in the above manner was in keeping with princely customs in those days, and the successful hero of a prince in the matter was considered to be a highly acclaimed hero. The three princesses carried away by Bhishma were named Amba, Ambika and Ambalika. The three were put in chains on the chariot. Amba with folded hands prayed to Bhishma to spare her as she had already mentally chosen Madra Raj as her life's partner. Hearing this Bhishma got into rage, because such a behaviour from a princess having a predetermined Svayamvara was unethical and unbecoming of a Kshatriya princess. He at once dropped Amba on the road and hurried towards Hastinapur with Ambika and Ambalika. Reaching Hastinapur Bhishma made a present of the two princesses to his half-brother King Vichitravirya, who was extremely happy at obtaining two queens at one stroke without having to do anything whatsoever in the bargain. But as a result of having to keep company of two queens at the same time the already weakling of a King became very weak further and soon died. After his death the young queens invoked the good offices of Veda Vyasa and through him begot two sons; a blind son by Ambika and a blond son by Ambalika. The former who was the elder of the two was named Dhrita Rashtra and the latter Pandu.

It may not be out of place to give a brief account at this stage of some antecedents of Veda Vyasa and of Satyavati. Dasa Raja, whose principal occupation was catching fish, one day cast his net in the river. To his great luck he netted a very big fish. After landing the big fish on the bank Dasa Raja opened its stomach. He was startled to find inside two human babies—a boy and a girl. Dasa Raja took them home and reared them up with care and affection. The girl was Satyavati who was known at that time as Matsya Gandha as she used to exude foul smell of fish from her body, having been in the stomach of the fish as a baby. She grew up into an otherwise exquisitely beautiful girl but Dasa Raja was extremely worried over her foul smell. He did not know what to do. At last he thought out a plan; he would keep her near a ferry Ghat of the river—a place used by every kind of people including sages endowed with supernatural powers. If the girl could attract any such person by virtue of her physical charms she might be cured of her fell disease by the grace of such a spiritual man. Accordingly Matsya Gandha was made to wait near a ferry to try her luck.

One day sage Parasara Muni crossed the river at the ferry Ghat. His eyes fell on the beautiful Matsya Gandha but he could not make out why such a young and beautiful girl was sitting at such an unusual place and alone. The sage approached the girl and asked her why she was there in such a manner. Matsya Gandha narrated her story of woe and affliction to the sage and implored his grace and kindness. The sage was moved by piety on hearing her story and was seized with compassion: He took the girl in a boat to a dark island (Krishna Dvip) which was enveloped in thick mist. There he impregnated her when she was cured completely of her foul smell. Instead she started exuding smell of lotus flowers. As a result of the union she gave birth to a son who was none other than Veda Vyasa, named Krishna Dvaipayan Vyasa—derived from the black island on which he was born. The name of Satyavati was also changed from Matsya Gandha (fish smelling) to Padma Gandha (lotus smelling.)

It is said that Ambika shut her eyes, out of fear when she saw Veda Vyasa; as a result the son that was born of the union was blind. On the other hand when Ambalika saw Veda Vyasa all her blood got dried up out of fear, and she became bloodless. Consequently the boy born of the union became blond, colourless. After the death of Vichitravirya the responsibility of running the kingdom fell entirely on Bhishma, who acted as something like the Regent. When the two sons by the two queens grew up problem of succession posed difficulties. As the elder of the two, the son by Ambika named Dhrita Rashtra would have succeeded to the office without any question but for his blindness. Hence the younger, the blond son by Ambalika named Pandu, ascended the throne. Pandu had two queens, Kunti and Madri; and these two queens gave him five sons—three by Kunti and two by Madri. Kunti, even before her marriage, learnt Mantras to successfully invoke gods. When trying to verify her Mantra before she had been married she attracted benedictions of the Sun and thereby gave birth to a son. As the child was born before she had been formally married the child was considered illegitimate. To hide her shame Kunti cast away her first born and was picked up and reared by a carpenter. This boy in later years became well known as the great Kaurava hero Karna. After marriage Kunti invoked one by one the gods Dharma Raj, Pavana the Wind god and the king of the gods Indra; and out of these unions were born Yudhisthir, Bhim and Arjun. Thus although all of them were unquestionably accepted as sons of King Pandu they were publicly referred to as Dharma Putra (son of Dharma), Pavana Nandan (son of Pavana) and Indra Suta (son of Indra). At fervent entreaties of Madri the Mantra was given to her by Kunti to be used only once. The crafty Madri used the Mantra to invoke the twin gods Asvini Kumaras and thereby begot twin sons Nakul and Sahadeva.

Dhrita Rashtra through his royal consort begot one hundred sons including Durjodhan, the eldest, and Duhshahsan. In deference to a curse Pandu often lived away from his kingdom, in the forest, and although the second queen invariably accompanied him he would not touch or fondle her. The curse was that he would succumb to death if he embraced a woman. But when the king was blessed with five sons born of his two queens Pandu forgot every thing else out of sheer joy and embraced his dear queen Madri. True to the augury King Pandu died as a result and queen Madri underwent self-immolation,—

committed Suttee,—on her husband's funeral pyre. The children who were still young now started being brought up along with the one hundred sons of Dhrita Rashtra. Kunti also mothered Nakul and Sahadev. Yudhishthir was not only the eldest son of the deceased king Pandu but was also the eldest among all the one hundred and five princes of the court of Hastinapur. According to custom and tradition Yudhishthir was the rightful claimant to the throne. Durjodhan, however, could not digest the idea of Yudhishthir becoming the king and he hated all the five Pandava brothers, the five sons of Pandu, from the core of his heart. Although he and his brothers numbered one hundred they were no match in prowess for two Pandavas—Bhim and Arjun. Bhim was physically the strongest among all the one hundred and five princes and Arjun was the most competent archer. Durjodhan hatched many conspiracies to do away with the Pandavas, specially Bhim, for good. But every one of his attempts failed. Under advice from other elders the Pandavas with their mother tried to keep a safe distance between them and Durjodhana. When Yudhishthir attained maturity his ascendance to the throne could no longer be delayed. Durjodhan, however, openly opposed this. He maintained that his father had been deprived from his rightful claim on the plea that he was blind; now he was the eldest son of the original rightful claimant, as such he should be declared king. But this demand could not be entertained and Yudhishthir was duly solemnised as the new king of Hastinapur.

Durjodhan was not reconciled. He resolved that when claim could not be accepted in the normal way he would fulfill his desire through conspiracy, intrigue, cheating or any means fair or foul. After careful planning he decided to challenge king Yudhishthir in a game of dice. With the collaboration of his maternal uncle Sakuni, the arch gambler and conspirator who possessed 'loaded' dice, Durjodhan succeeded in defeating the king in the game. In the process Yudhishthir lost all his possession. In the long run he had to leave his kingdom, in terms of the wager, and go to banishment for twelve years, the last one of which was to be incognito. His brothers and the common wife Draupadi accompanied him. Being successful by such unethical and despicable means to grab the throne of Hastinapur, although temporarily for twelve years, Durjodhan decided to establish himself as the permanent King. When the Pandavas returned after successfully carrying out the obligations and claimed back the throne for Yudhishthir Durjodhan flatly refused. He declared that he would not give up the throne or any part of land of the kingdom even of the size of the needle-head without a fight. Ultimately the issue had to be taken to the battle field of Kuru-Kshetra where rulers of all principalities in India participated in one or the other side. Sri Krishna, a relation and friend of the family, personally sided with the Pandavas but placed his crack army at the disposal of the Kauravas. Further he announced that although he would be with the Pandavas he would not take up arms; he acted as the charioteer of the Pandava hero Arjun. When, as desired by Arjun he took the chariot in between the opposing armies arraigned in battle formation before the actual battle started, Arjun was emotionally bent down seeing that the persons he was required to slay were the ones without whom life and living in the world would be meaningless. At this he said he would not fight. Leaving his famous bow—Gandiva—he sat silently seized with grief and remorse. Sri Krishna at this time addressed him to shake off his remorse and grief and temporary diffidence. What was said on that occasion constitutes the priceless gift of the Shrimad Bhagvad Gita.

For the 'Spiritual Interpretation' one has to penetrate deeper into the fabric of the Mahabharata story and decipher the imageries used in the book in the shape of different names of the heroes and the heroines.

One of Swami Sri Yukteshvar's important advises was that one should endeavour to find out meanings of core-words of the Gita in the body of the Gita itself; that the meanings of such words available in the Gita would be in the correct context of the message of the Gita. Another important instruction of the Swami was that before undertaking study of the Gita one should acquire basic knowledge in Samkhya and Patanjal philosophies. How valuable these advises were could be realised only after a thorough study of the holy book. The first Chapter which according to Sri Yukteshvar is the introductory part of the book, contains the relevant features and imageries that can lead to the unfolding of the underlying meanings of the Gita. Hence it is advisable to take up discussion of the Gita chapter-wise.

Excellence of the Gita

The Gita as mentioned earlier is a splendid treatise on Yoga. It may be argued that almost all its themes are based on different principles of Yoga. Instructions and teachings contained in this wonderful book cover all the Hindu basic concepts of creation and of life and living. Through explanations in the Samkhya, Karma and, Jnana Yoga chapters the Gita has laid down the most profound arguments in respect of intellectually determining what is Real and what are Apparent, specifying the principles of the Spirit, the Chaitanya or Pursusha, in relation to the apparent 'forms'. It has described and clarified the principles underlying the conceptions of 'Karma,' 'Dharma' and the Yuga. Various types of Yajnas, holy work, have been described which may be employed for attaining Yoga or 'link' with the Self. The Fifth Chapter of the book describes the essential features of correct renunciation, Sannyas.

The Sixth Chapter, the Dhyana or the Abhyasa Yoga, constitutes the most Illuminating and practical aspect for attainment of Yoga.

Among the different Yajnas or holy work advocated by the Gita the one referring to the controlling of the incoming and the out-going breaths, the technique of sacrificing of the one into the other, very correctly expounds the basic feature of Pranayama as advocated in the system of Kriya Yoga.

Arjuna Vishāda Yoga, Or Sainya Darshana Yoga

The first chapter of any Sanskrit literature is to be considered as the introduction to the subject matter of discussion of the book, Swami Sri Yukteshvar used to emphasise. There was no custom in olden days of adding a separate chapter on introduction in Sanskrit literature. As such the first chapter of the Gita is required to be studied carefully to grasp the trend of discussion in the book proper, and endeavour to decipher the imageries of the story.

The very first verse of this chapter contains two very significant words which 'hide' within them the basis of the message of the Gita. The very first two words of the verse are (1) Dharma Kshetra and (2) Kuru Kshetra. The verse reads:

> *"Assembled in battle array in Dharmakshetra Kurukshetra what did my Sons and Sons of Pandu do Oh! Sanjaya?"

> *"Dharma Kshetre Kuru Kshetre Samavetā Yuyutsavah Māmakā Pāndavāschaiva Kimakurvata Sanjaya." (I, 1)

In the two worlds there is a common component 'Kshetra' which has been separately qualified by the components 'Dharma' and 'Kuru'. Kshetra means 'field' but what has been indicated by the word 'field' in the context of the message of the Gita has to be carefully considered. The commonly understood meaning is that KuruKshetra was a battle field on which a battle for assertion of righteousness over the un-righteous had been raged; between forces of righteousness represented by the Pandavas and the forces of unrighteousness represented by the Kauravas. By adopting the advice of Sri Yukteshvar, when one goes over the pages and chapters of the Gita he is rewarded with the contextual meaning of the word 'Kshetra' in the definition obtained in the thirteenth chapter.

> "Prakriti and Purusha are (Kshetra) the Field and (Kshetrajna) Knower of the Field."*

*"Prakritim Purushamchaivah Kshetram Kshetrajnamevacha" (XIII, 1)

The 'field' has been further defined as follows:

"This body, Oh son of Kunti, is called the Field."**

**"Idam Sariram Kaunteya Kshetramityabhidhiyate" (XIII, 2)

"The Five great elements (Mahabhuta,) the Ego, the Intelligence, the Primeval Prakriti, the Ten organs (of senses and action), the eleventh (mind), the Five Objects (Tanmatras), Desire, Aversion, Joy, Sorrow, Death, Consciousness and Existence—these in a nutshell are called the Field (Kshetra) and its ramifications."***

***"Mahābhutanyahamkaro Buddhiravyakamevacha Indriyāni Dashaikancha Pancha Chendriyagocharāh Ichchhā Dveshah Sukham Dukham Samghātaschetana Dhritih Etat Kshetram Samāsena Savikāramudāhritam." (XIII, 6 & 7)

One would get an idea of what kind of a battle as described in the epic was fought from the above definition of Kshetra or the field. When the imageries in the story of the Mahabharata are deciphered the correct nature of its themes can properly be comprehended.

The Mahabharata story starts with king Santanu and his two queens, Ganga and Satyavati. It will be interesting to find that these actually represent imageries of the basic conceptions of the scheme of creation as contained in the Samkhya philosophy. Samkhya lays down that there are three fundamental Principles; (1) the Param Purusha, (2) Purusha and (3) Prakriti. Param Purusha is the Spirit without beginning and end and the Only Real Substance that exists; Purusha and Prakriti are but its Spiritual (Chaitanya) and Material (Jada) aspects respectively. Purusha is the Chaitanya that 'lies' within every 'being' or 'form' in the creation. Prakriti is defined as the state of equilibrium of three Gunas—Sattva (Sentient), Raja (Kinetic or Mutative) and Tama (Static). Thus the Purusha and the Prakriti are not separate from Param Purusha and are but part and parcel of Param Purusha the Omnipresent, Omniscient, Limitless Spirit—the One without a second. The Universal scene, creation, has been said to be the result of chains of deformation of the original Prakriti under the 'impact' of the Spirit according to Samkhya postulates. Swami Sri Yukteshvar, while explaining this phenomenon; referred to the behaviour of iron filings when placed in an electro-magnetic field.

Iron filings are magnetic materials; a magnetic material is defined as having been composed of molecular magnets. It has been scientifically observed that when these iron filings are placed in a magnetic field they behave like magnets. It is explained that the molecular magnets in a magnetic material are arranged in such a manner that their poles get neutralised among themselves thereby negating magnetic effects of the molecules and remaining in a state of equilibrium. As soon as the material comes close to a magnet its molecular magnets are subjected to magnetic effects of the actual magnet and the molecular magnets get rearranged like in any actual magnet. The case of Prakriti is also likewise; the Chaitanya or the Spirit 'influences' or shines 'on' it causing disequilibrium in its state of 'poise' when the self-satisfied Gunas are disturbed and they get 'precipitated.' When this results it is known as 'deformation' or Vikriti. The very first stage of deformation is called Mahat, or the Mahat Tattva in terms of the Twenty four principles of creation of Samkhya. The Gita has described the 'Mahat' as the 'womb' of the creation scheme, as the scene of creation starts with further deformation of the Mahat Tattva.

Samkhya observes that the Mahat Tattva quickly gets deformed further manifesting Ahamkar Tattva, the Ego, bringing about idea of separation in the indivisible-Absolute, with the concomitant manifestation of intelligence, Buddhi or Sattva-Buddhi which may be compared with the positive pole of a magnet, and the Mind, the Manas, Tama Guna or Anandatva which is comparable to a magnet's negative pole. Of the three Gunas the Raja is the active principle, which by its actions manifests Sattva Buddhi. With the manifestation of Buddhi its negative complement, the mind, also gets manifested. Sattva Buddhi or Buddhi constitutes the positive pole Sattva Guna of the 'polarised' Prakriti if it is taken as a magnetised magnetic material; the Manas, Tama Guna the negative pole and the active principle Raja the neutral pole. Sri Yukteshvar termed this Raja Guna as the neutralising pole as this is the most powerful among the three Gunas having the capacity to neutralise the two extreme poles. The 'polarised' Prakriti is thus provided with Sattva, Raja and Tama Gunas together with their intermediate stages of Sattva-Raja and Raja-Tama. These five kinds of the Gunas form the very base of creation, and are called the Pancha Tattva. These five principles are considered to constitute the Causal Body, the Karana Sharira of the Purusha. Each of the above five are but conglomerates again of the same three Gunas in differing proportions. On further deformation, out of the five Sattva Guna components of the above five principles evolve the five senses, the *Pancha Jnanendriya*, aggregate of which is the *Mind*. In the same way out of the five Raja Guns components evolve the five organs of action, the *Pancha Karmendriya*; and out of the five Tama components evolve the five subtle objects, *Pancha Tanmatra*. The aggregate of the five Raja components that evolve the *Karmendriyas*, is called *Prana*. The process of deformation of Prakriti comes to an end with the Tanmatras getting further deformed into gross matters, the five fundamental elements or the *Pancha Mahabhuta*. The five fundamental elements of gross matter together constitute the *Gross Material Body, Sthula Sharira* of Purusha. The five Jnanendriyas, five Karmendriyas, five Tanmatras together with Mind, Intelligence and Ego constitute the *Fine Material Body, Sukshma Sharira*, of the Purusha.

Mahabharata Imageries

To prove that Mahabharata is an imagery, the names of its heroes and heroines may be subjected to etymological derivation. They are as follows:

Santanu: Samam (Unchanged, unruffled) Tanum (Body, form, features) Yasya, Sa (He, whose); the Time-less, Ripple-less, Ever Existent, Overlord. Thus King Santanu be taken to represent the Param Purusha postulate of Samkhya. As the Param Purusha has two aspects—the Chaitanya and Jada aspects, the two queens of Santanu of the epical story Ganga and Satyavati are shown as his consorts.

Gangā: Gang (Brahmandam, the Universe) Gachhati (Goes, Permeates,) Ya, Se (That, Which); that which remains permeating the universe,—the Chaitanya or Purusha aspect of the Param Purusha.

Satyavati: Satyam (Chaitanyam, Spirit) Vartate (Dwells, Shines) Yasyām (on whom). The Chaitanya shining or by exercising 'impact' on the primeval Prakriti results in its deformation causing manifestation of chain of creation. That the story of the Mahabharata is the story of the progenies of Satyavati confirms the Samkhya postulate that creation occurs due to deformation (Vikriti) of Prakriti in the presence of Purusha.

Thus all the three elder actors in the story of the epic are found to conform to the three ultimate principles as laid down in the Samkhya philosophy. The imagery does not rest there, but extends to subsequent details.

Chitrāngada: Chitrita (Colored, Painted, Disfigured) Anga (Body, Form, Characteristics) Yasya Se (He, Whose). Chitrangada is the first son of Satyavati by King Santanu. But he did not live long. Under Samkhya the primeval Prakriti first gets 'deformed' (Vikriti) with the impact of Chaitanya producing Mahat Tattva, a stage that quickly changes into Ahamakara by further deformation. Chitrangada is thus analogous to Mahat Tattva of Samkhya.

Vichitra Veerya: Vichitra (Strange, Variegated, Peculiar) Veerya (Prowess) Yasya, Se (He, Who has). Although a weaking Vichitra Veerya ascended the throne of Hastinapur and was responsible for making the dynastic line continue, a strange but significant capacity. In Samkhya postulates this conforms to the Ahamkara or the Ego principle which by manifesting Intelligence and Mind begins building up the Fine Material Body, the Sukshma Sharira of Purusha.

Pāndu: Pandu means absence of pigment; colourless, untarnished, pure. Pandu of the epic was the son of Vichitra Veerya by Ambālikā, the determining and affirming component of Intelligence, *Nishchayātmikā Buddhi*. It compares with *Sattva Buddhi or Buddhi* of Samkhya exposition.

Dhrita Rāshtra: Dhritam (Held) Rāshtram (Kingdom, the Apparent Universal Scene) Yena (by whom); that which maintains the idea of existence of the scene of creation, and thus keeps the Reality 'covered up' beyond the ken of comprehension. The description coincides with the definition of *Mind, Anandattva or Enjoyment* of Samkhya. Powers of the mind are very strong but they lack discretion or power to distinguish between the truth and otherwise and hence figuratively termed as blind.

Before dealing with the other progenies of Satyavati it may be worthwhile at this stage to discuss about the sons of Gangā. It may be recalled that Ganga had thrown seven of her new-born sons into the river and they lay immersed in the waters of the Ganga. The eighth son was Deva Vrata who later became famous as Bhishma. It has been shown above that Ganga represents Purusha, the Chaitanya or the Spirit aspect of Param Purusha in creation. Progenies of the Ganga have therefore of necessity to belong to the realm of the Spirit. The Universal scene is created on Prakriti as the base in the presence of Chaitanya by getting serially

'deformed.' But there can be no creation without the presence of Chaitanya and that at every stage. It has been seen in the foregoing in the gradual emergence of the various 'scenes' of creation how Causal, Fine Material and Gross Material Bodies of Purusha are formed. Deformation or Vikriti that takes place in the Prakriti in the presence of Purusha or Chaitanya is the effect of the Divine Maya. The Spirit or the Purusha is present at every stage of creation described above and a name has been ascribed notionally to the Spirit that is present at every stage.

In philosophical parlance two words are very commonly used—Samashti and Vyashti. Samashti is the Collective and Vyashti the Unit. Thus the forest of trees is the collective while every individual tree of the forest represents the unit. Using these two expressions in the matter of the 'In-Dwelling' (Purusha) Spirit in various forms of creation we get the following result.

The Chaitanya in the collective Causal Body, Karana Sharira of the Purusha, is known as the *Isvara* and Chaitanya in every Unit of the Causal Body is called *Prājna*. Similarly the Chaitanya in the collective Fine Material Body, Samashti Sukshma Sharira of the Purusha, is called *Hiranya Garbha*, and the Spirit in every Unit of Fine Material Body or Vyashti Sukshma Sharira is called *Vaisvānara*; while the Chaitanya in the Samashti Sthula Sharira is known as *Virāt* and the same in the Vyashti Sthula Sharira is called *Vishva*. Thus what are Isvara, Hiranya Garbha and Virāt in the collective or Samashti sense of the in-dwelling spirit are Prājna, Vaisvānara and Vishva in the Vyashti or Unit sense. Isvara and Prājna jointly constitute what is conceived as God *Vishnu*, Hiranya Garbha and Vaishvānara constitute *Brahm*ā and Virat and Visva jointly constitute *Mahesvara*the Protector, Creator and Destroyer,—the Divine Trinity,—of the Hindu pantheon.

The Chaitanya that lies permeating through every bit of creation like the string that runs through the beads in a necklace, making it possible for the beads to maintain the form of the necklace, is called *Kutastha Chaitanya*. It is also known as the *Sutrātmā. Every form and particle in the creation becomes possible of cognition due to the presence of this Chaitanya in it. Without Kutastha Chaitanya nothing in creation would have been comprehensible. All the aforementioned, notionally designated, Chaitanyas are beyond human comprehension being part and parcel of the Ever-Existent and the All Pervasive Chaitanya. The seven sons of Ganga who remain immersed in her waters represent the above notionally designated seven Chaitanyas. The eighth son Deva Vrata, Bhishma, is also an imagery and belongs to the realm of the Spirit. Bhishma, according to the epic, did*

not himself rule the kingdom, himself did not become king, although it was due to his presence that everything went on smoothly in the kingdom. He was, as it were, a witness to the running of the kingdom. As such this last son of Ganga may be said to represent the Sākshi Chaitanya of the Hindu philosophies. This is also known as the *Abhāsa Chaitanya*, reflection of the *Kutastha Chaitanya* and manifested by virtue of the *Kutastha Chaitanya*. It is the power of 'seeing'—the Drishi,—which identifying with the 'seen' or to be seen—the Drishya,—transforms into what is designated in Samkhya as *Asmitā*.

What have been discussed above show that the story of the epic is a splendid allegory. The remaining actors and actresses in the great drama will also be 'seen' when deciphered, as imageries of important basic spiritual conceptions of the Hindu culture.

To go back to the first verse of the first chapter:

It can be stated now that the first two words in the first verse of the chapter indicating the 'field,' referred to as Kshetra, as the human body or 'form' placed in the broad perspective of the background formed by the series of deformations of the Prakriti and their actions and interactions. It is the *Chaitanya*, the *Purusha*, which is the knower of the *Kshetra* and its upholder. The human body is the field of performance, the Kuru Kshetra, for spiritual efforts to overcome the obstacles that stand in the way and attain the Spirit, which tantamounts to identification with the Chaitanya. The deformations of the Prakriti and its ramifications in the presence of the Spirit offer the broad back-ground, the Dharma Kshetra, the Spirit being the actual holder of the field, the Dharma.

Men suffer from delusion and grief because of losing awareness of the Spirit in and all around; hence re-establishment of Self in the Spirit is the secret of overcoming all sorrow. In the interpretations given above Pāndavas are the derivatives of Intelligence, the Buddhi, which helps in manifesting the Truth, the Spirit; and Kauravas, the progenies of the Mind that produce cover over the Spirit. Every aspirant after attaining the Spirit, which is equivalent to achieving emancipation, has to face up to the inherent conflict between the above two opposite forces; and hence every *Sādhaka* has his own 'Kuru Kshetra' battle to encounter.

Hence the combatants on the two sides have also to be considered in appropriate light in conformity with what has been given out so far. The following verses of the chapter give names of these combatants. These verses were spoken by Durjodhan, the eldest Kaurava, to Dronacharya, the teacher of the princes of the palace of Hastinapur, who had to agree to fight on his side having been on his pay.

"Look, Oh teacher! at the disposition of the mighty army of the sons of Pāndu arrayed by the son of Drupada, your celebrated disciple."*

*"PasyaitānPānduputrānām Achārya Mahatim Chamum Vyudhām Drupadaputrena Tava Sishyena Dhimatā."

"Here are determined archers on great chariots who are equal in combat power to that of Bhim and Arjun such as Yuyudhan, Virat, Drupada;**

**"Atra Surāh Mahesvāsā Bhimārjunasamā Yudhih Yuyudhāna Virātascha Drupadascha Mahārathāh"

"Dhrishtaketu, Chekitan, Kashiraj the strong. Purujit, Kuntibhoj, Shaivya—Oh! the great among men;"***

***"Dhrishtaketuschekitāna Kāsirājascha Veeryavān Purujit Kuntibhojascha Shaivyascha Narapungavah"

"The virile Yudhamanyu, Vikranta, Uttamauja and sons of Draupadi and of Subhadrā, all of whom are great fighters."****

*****"Yudhāmanyuscha Vikrānta Uttamaujāscha Veeryavān Saubhadra Draupadeyāscha Sarva Eva Mahārathāh" (I—3, 4,5,6)

The above heroes are all on the side of the Pandavas. The following verse gives names of the eminent heroes on the side of the Kauravas:

"Thou, Bhishma, Karna, Kripa, Samitinjaya Ashvatthāmā, Vikarna, Saumadatti and similar others."*

*"Bhavān Bhishmascha Karnascha Kripascha Samitinjaya Asvatthāmā Vikarnascha Saumadattistathaivacha." (I—8)

When the names of the above combatants are subject to etymological derivation there will be no doubt that the names have been carefully and dexterously coined to make them properly fit in with the imagery the narration have been intended to be. Each name, it will be found, stands for a specific attribute as found in the Pātanjal philosophy. The case of Bhishma has already been deciphered above. It has to be kept in mind that the 'battle-field' and the fight is a novel one, between the helpful urges of the definitive Intelligence and the unbalancing forces of the propensities, the actual fight being performance of Pranayam or the Kriya Yoga.

Starting with the collaborators of the Pandavas we have:

Drupadaputra: (Dhrishtadyumna): Dhrishta (as a result of rubbing, friction) Dyumna (illumination, light); light that is generated by rubbing or by friction. The illumination within that results by the friction of breaths while performing Pranayam.

Yuyudhāna: Yoddhum (to fight) Ishāna (determined); the one who is determined to fight. Thus it is equivalent to what is described as Shraddhā in Patanjal.

*Uttamauj*ā: Uttama (excellent) Ojah (vigour) Yasya Sa (he, who has); that which makes for vigour; which is another name for *Veerya*.

Chekitāna: Derived from 'Chiketi'—Chiketi (to know); that which knows. Thus it is *Smriti*.

Virāt: Visheshena (distinctively) Rājate (revels); revelling in a distinctive manner. It is one way of describing Samādhi.

Kāshirāja: Karshayan (collecting, gathering) Rājate (stays); act of remembering, the word expresses the significance of *Prajnā*.

Drupada: Drutam (speedy, quick) Pada (steps, progress) Yasya Sa (he, whose); he or that which is speedy; *Tivra Vega*.

Dhrishtaketu: Dhrishyate (smashes, destroys) Ketava (obstacles) Yena (by whom, by which); by which the obstacles are destroyed. This refers to *Yama* of Pātanjal Yoga Sutras.

Shaivya: Pertaining to Shiva (well being); *Niyama*.

Kuntibhoja: Kuntim (powers of attracting spiritual experiences) Bhunakti (eats, characteristics of) Ya Sa (he, who); characteristics of which are attracting spiritual experiences; *Asana*.

Yudhādmanyu: Yoddhum (to fight, in performing) Manyu (engaged) Ya Sa (he, who); remaining engaged in fight or endeavour; in performing Prānāyam.

Purujit: Paurān (Dwellers of 'town' or 'locality') Jayati (Overcomes, Conquers); conquering of the dwellers of Pura, town or dwelling; conquering the senses; reversal of the direction of senses making them powerless; the Pratyāhāra.

Saubhadra (Subhadrā's son): Abhimanyu: Abhi (from all directions) Manute (manifests); total manifestation. To the Yogis this is the combined stage of Dhāranā or Smriti, Dhyāna and Samādhi, called *Samyama*.

Draupadeyāh: Sons of Draupadi. Drupada has been deciphered as speedy or quick-footed; Draupadi, hence, is what is generated or produced by the speedy; her sons—productions by Draupadi; manifestations by virtue of what is produced by the speedy. Draupadi, it will be seen later, is Kundalini Shakti; her sons are the manifestations caused in the five chakras in the Shushumna while Kundalini is roused.

It will be interesting to find that what has been established above by dissecting the various names of the heroes on the Pandava side actually conform to essential edicts of the Pātanjal Yoga Sutras. Some of these are quoted below before pointing to the identical meanings.

"For others (through observation of) Shraddha, Veerya Smriti, Samādhi and Prajnā."*

*"Sraddhā Veerya Smriti Samādhi Prajnāpurvakam Itareshām." (Samādhipad, 20)

"(Success) is imminent for the quick-footed."**

**"Tivra Samvegānām Asannā." (Samādhipad, 21)

"Ignorance is the cause for this."***

***"Tasya Heturavidyā." (Sādhanapād 24)

"In its absence there is absence of link which is equivalent to annihilation; realisation of this is emancipation."#

#"Tadabhāvāt Samyogābhāvo Hānantaddrishte Kaivalyam." (Sādhanpād, 25)

"Means for annihilation is unwavering and undisturbed Vivekakhyāti".##

##"Vivekakhyātiraviplavā Hānopāya" (Sādhanpād, 26)

"Effulgence of .Jnāna at the destruction of impurity by performing Yoga steps is Vivekakhyāti."###

###"Yogānganushthānāt　Ashuddhikshaye　Jnānadiptirvivekakhyāti." (Sādhanpād, 28)

"Observance of 'don'ts and do's,' assuming proper posture of sitting, practising of controlling the breaths, attaining withdrawal of the senses, gaining subtle memory, continuing to maintain the realisation and complete concentration are the eight steps of Yoga."*

*"Yamaniyamāsana Prānāyāma Pratyāhārā Dhārana Dhyāna Samādhayorashtāvangāni" (Sādhanpād, 29)

"The three together is Samyama"**

**"Trayorekatra Samyama" (Vibhutipād, 4)

The views expressed earlier that the various combatants in the epical battle were but different formulations of the Yoga Sutras may therefore be taken to be justified. The same argument will apply, it will be seen, in the case of combatants on the side of the Kauravas. The names of these heroes are as follows:

Drona, Bhishma, Karna, Kripa, Samitinjaya, Ashvatthāmā, Vikarna and Saumadatti. What Bhishma stands for has already been explained.

Drona: Drona—Karmanām Dravibhāva ('Fluid' impressions of Karma—work); lasting impressions of work or performances; effects of work that lasts or lingers, which is equivalent to *Sanskār*.

Karna: Karanashila Iti, (work that is deemed to be duty, and one has great attraction for such work); this sounds akin to *Rāga* of the Yoga Sutras.

Vikarna: Viparita Karna (opposite of Attraction, Aversion); which is *Dvesha* in terms of Yoga Sutras.

Samitinjaya: *Jayadratha*: Jayati (Controls, Conquers) Ramitva (By penetration, Attachment); it is evident that the word is used to express figuratively *Abhinivesh* in the formulations of Pātanjal.

*Somadatti, son of Somadatta = Bhurishrav*ā: Bhurim (Extensive, Endless) Shravam (Oozings, Fluid impressions); it conforms to the description of *Karma* or work which begets more and more Karma.

*Ashvatth*ā*mā*: Ashvan (Collecting, Gathering) Tishthati (remains, Sticks); son of Drona, and as such considered as after effects of Sanskār, which is desire—*Vāsanā or Ashay*.

Kripa: Krip (To contemplate, Imagine) 'A' (Contrarily, Wrongly); this is another way of describing delusion or *Avidy*ā of Pātanjal.

Bhishma: has been interpreted above already; it conforms to the formulation of *Asmit*ā.

The following quotations from the Pātanjal Yoga Sutras will show that these formulations actually refer to as the above 'combatants.'

> "Ignorance, Identity of Self with the Seen (Drishi and Drishya); Desire, Aversion and Penetrative Attachment are the five Obstacles."*
>
> *"Avidyā Asmitā Rāga Dvesha Abhinivesha Pancha Kleshā." (Sādhanpād, 3)
>
> "Isvara is a Special In-Dweller (which is) untouched by Obstacles, Work, Wrong Ideas and Desires."**
>
> **"Klesha Karma Vipāka Ashayayair Aparāmrishta Purusha Visesha Isvara." (Samādhipād, 24)
>
> "Identity of power of seeing with sight is Asmita."***

***"Drikdarshanashaktyorekatmāivasmitā." (Sādhanpād, 6)

"Rāga is that which follows happiness."#

#"Sukhānushayee Rāga." (Sādhanpād, 7)

"Dvesha is reaction to aversion."##

##"Dukhānushayee Dvesha." (Sādhanpād, 8)

"Pleasant feeling that binds even the wise to the 'form' or body is Abhinivesha."###

###"Svarasavāhividushohpi Tanvanubandho Abhinivesha." (Sādhanpād, 9)

Interpretation of the important combatants as given out in the introduction to the Gita, in the First Chapter, will be complete after estimates are worked out about the five Pāndavas, their wife Draupadi and her sons, about their friend and benefactor Sree Krishna and about Durjodhan, the eldest son of Dhrita Rāshtra.

The front side of the human body, to the Yogis, is the Rāshtra, the kingdom—which is the 'domain' of the mind. The vertebral region at the back is what is said to be 'away' from the kingdom. There are one hundred principal Nādis, nerves, spread over the front; while the most important Nādi in the human system, the Shushumnā, runs through the middle of the vertebral column, with Idā and Pingalā running parallel to it along its left and right respectively. It is said that sixty thousand subsidiary Nādis emanate from the above three principal Nādis and spread over the entire body making every part of the body conscious.

Pingala is the 'seat' of the Sun principle; the Nādis that emanate from Pingalā are said to belong to the Solar Dynasty, Surya Vansha. Idā is the seat of the Moon principle, and Nādis arising from it are considered to belong to the Lunar Dynasty, Chandra Vansha. Shushumnā is the seat of Intelligence, Buddhi; Idā and Pingalā are considered as but reflectlons of Shushumnā, which 'rules' over all the Nadis. Nadis that arise out of Shushumnā are said to belong to Vrishni Vansha to which Sree Krishna belonged. The word Vrishni means 'that which lords it over.' The above three dynasties have been mentioned as the most famous ruling families in the Mahabharata.

It has been shown that Pandu represents Intelligence, Buddhi, and hence Shushumnā is its seat in the body, which is 'away from the kingdom.' Shushumnā is considered in two parts; from the region opposite the navel upwards which is the Upper, and the other that is downwards from the region opposite the navel which is the Lower. The Upper part represents the elder queen of Pandu of the epical story which has the capacity for 'inviting' Spiritual experiences and hence called Kunti (Kun=to invite). The Lower part represents the second queen Mādri. Shushumnā is distinguished by having five centres within it which are considered as seats of the Spirit; three centres are in the Upper part and two in the Lower. Those in the upper are (i) Opposite the navel, (ii) Opposite the heart and (iii) Opposite the throat. In the lower part we have one (iv) Opposite the generative organ and the other (v) Opposite the anus. Above the aforementioned five centres is one in the region (vi) in between the eyebrows within. These six centres are known to the Yogis as the Sat Chakras, the six centres of spiritual experience, the first five of which are considered as seats of the Five Fundamental Principles, Pancha Tattva.

Pāndavas: The five sons of Pandu; Yudhishthir, Bhim, Arjun, Nakul and Sahadev; the first three are considered as sons by Kunti and the other two sons of Mādri.

Yudhishthir: Yudhi (In combat) Sthir (Steady); Steadiness in combat; represents the first of the five Tattvas, the *Vyoma Tattva*—the Akasha or the Space Principle. The Chakra is Opposite throat and is called the Vishuddha.

Bhim: The second Chakra, in the region of Shushumnā opposite the heart and is known as *Anāhata Chakra*; it is the seat of the *Marut Tattva*—the Air principle. It represents the second son of Pandu by Kunti, the wonder worker (Bhima Karmā) Bhim.

Arjun: The third Chakra, the one in the region of the Shushumnā opposite the navel, which is known as the *Manipur Chakra* and considered to be the seat of *Vahnni Tattva*—Fiery principle. This 'principle' or Tattva is the most potent and powerful of the five principles that constitute the Causal Body. It represents the greatest of the Pandava heroes, Arjun.

Nakul: The Fourth Chakra, the centre in the region of Shushumnā opposite the generative organ, is the seat of *Jala Tattva*—Water Principle of the Pancha Tattva. It is represented in the epical account as Nakula, son of Mādri. The Chakra is named *Svādhishthān*.

Sahadev: The Fifth and the last of the five Chakras, in the region of the Shushumnā opposite the anus, is the seat of *Kshiti Tattva*—the Solid Principle. It is represented in the story as the second son by Mādri, Sahadev. The Chakra is named *Mulādhār*.

The foregoing completes the description of imageres of the five sons of Pāndu—the Pancha Pandavas. Their common wife was Draupadi, the daughter of Drupada. Another Pāndava celebrity on the side of the Pandavas is Dhrishta Dyumna who, it has been mentioned above, had arraigned the huge Pāndava army in battle formations. Dhrishta Dyumna was the son of Drupada; as such Draupadi was his sister. He was trained in the art of war by Drona.

From the composition of the opposing forces, as narrated above, the nature of conflict alluded to in the Gita becomes apparent. The fight in the conflict also refers to proper work, Holy work—Yajna, in the holy book; the 'field' of performance having been defined as the body the holy work is evidently Pranayama, of 'sacrificing' the out-going breath into the in-coming breath' and vice-versa thereby stopping the flow of both. In the Pātanjal it has been laid down that success in the efforts after Prānāyāma is imminent to him that performs it with intensity. Two developments take place in the performer of Pranayama with intensity; due to 'rubbing' of the two currents of breaths,— the in-coming and the out-going, a brilliant white light manifests within the brain above Shushumnā, at about the Medulla Oblongata in between the eyebrows. The Yogis call this light as Body-Electricity, Deha Jyoti, which heralds the starting of spiritual experiences to the performer. The second development is what is known to the Yogis as 'awakening of the Kundalini'. The Yoga Sashtras teach that by quickening the pace of Pranayama for sustained and long periods the Kundalini Shakti or the Serpent Power that is supposed to lie dormant at the base of the Shushumnā, is awakened which then rises upwards from Chakra to Chakra manifesting appropriate experiences at every Chakra. The characters analysed give the following picture.

Dhrista Dyumna: Dhrista (Being rubbed; As a result of friction) Dyumna (light); light generated by friction in the process of Pranayam, *Deha Jyoti*; light generated within the body.

Draupadi: *Daughter of Drupada*: Kundalini Shakti; Serpent Power awakened as a result of quick performance of Pranayam.

Draupadeyāh: *Sons of Draupadi*: As Kundalini Shakti rises from Chakra to Chakra specks of various hue appear at the different Chakras; each speck is called a Vindu, and together they are called *Vindara*.

Dujodhan: *First son of Dhrita Rashtra*: Duh (Painful, Sorrowful) Yodhana (fight) Yasya Sa (He, Whose); he whose performance is sorrowful, conceited. This conceit, *Abhimān, is a great obstacle in spiritual progress.*

The remaining character to be deciphered in the grand drama is Sree Krishna, the Divine Propounder of the message of the Gita. It has already been stated that while he himself joined the Pandavas in the battle, but vouching that he would not hold arms and agreed only to drive Arjun's chariot, he supplied his crack army to the Kauravas.

Sree Krishna: Sree ('S'signifies good luck; 'R' is the Vahnni Veej—seed of fire; 'EE' signifies Power, Force) Krishna (Dark Colour); the luminant dark spot embedded inside a brilliantly white ball of light that manifests in between the eye-brows, at the Sixth Chakra, the Kutastha. In the Kriya Yoga system the Guru reveals this to the disciple as a part of routine of initiation. Sree Krishna has been variously designated as Adhi Yajna, Purushottama, Kutastha Chaitanya and Sutrātmā.

In the first chapter there are also accounts of blowing of battle conches by the Pāndavas and other heroes which when deciphered confirm the true 'Character' of the heroes as already described.

> "Rishikesha (the lord of senses, Sree Krishna,) blew Pānchajanya; Dhananjay (Arjun) blew Devadatta and Vrikodar (Bhim), the wonder Performer, blew the great conch Paundra."*

> *"Pānchjanyam Rishikesa Devadatta Dhananjaya Paundram Dadhmau Mahāsankham Bhimakarmā Vrikodara." (I, 15)

> "King Yudhishthir the son of Kunti, Ananta Vijay, Nakula and Sahadeva Sughosh and Manipushpak."**

> **"Ananta Vijayam Rājā Kunti putra Yudhishthira Nakula Sahadevascha Sughosha Manipushpakau." (I, 16)

> "Great fighters Kashiraj, Shikhandi and Dhrishta Dyumna and Virat and the unconquerable Satyaki," "Drupada and sons of Draupadi—all rulers of kingdoms; The great hero, the son of Subhadrā (Abhimanyu) blew their separate conches."***

> ***"Kāsyascha Paramesvashah Sikhandi Cha Mahārathā Drishta Dyumna Virātascha Sātyakischa Aparājita" "Drupada Draupadeyāscha Sarvasah Prithivipateh Saubhadrascha Mahāvāhuh Sankham Dadhmu Prithāk Prithak." (I, 17 & 18)

The above quoted verses indicate the inner revelations to the Yogi as he reaches deeper and deeper stages in the path of Yoga. The revelations relate to manifestation of the 'unutterable' sound Pranava that emanates as an unbroken stream submerging gradually physical attributes of the body. The sounds mentioned as blowing of conches by five Pandavas and by Sree

Krisnna refer to the manifestation of this sound from the different Chakras in the Shushumnā. The gradual refinement of the sound indicate deeper concentrations achieved. The sounds are taken as manifestation of resonance of the Tattvas or Principles that constitute the Causal Body, Karana Sharira, of Purusha.

As the mind withdraws gradually from the senses as a result of deep concentration an unusual buzzing note emanates, 'flowers out' as suggested in the Gita by the word Manipushpak, and becomes audible—which heralds achievement of the first stage of concentration. It appears as the sound of a bunch of disturbed blackbees (Matta Bhringa) arising out of Kshiti Tattva at the Muladhar Chakra, allegorically stated as the sound of *Mani Pushpak*, the conch of Sahadeva. When this sound manifests confusion arises as to whether this is the signal of revelation of the Pranava; hence the intensity of concentration at this stage is called '*Savitarka Samprajñāta Samādhi*'—concentration mixed with confusion and doubt.

By diving deeper into the buzzing sound like that of black-bees the Yoga performer gets elevated into the next Chakra, the Svadhishthān, which is the seat of Jala Tattva, when the sound becomes clearer and finer appearing like a note from the flute (*Vanshi Dhvani*). Svādhishthan, the seat of Jala Tattva, is represented in the story as Nakula. As the emanating sound becomes more clear (*Sughosha*) the clearer sound has been considered and given the name Sughosha. The quality of concentration improves dispelling the confusion of the earlier stage. It is called *Savichār Samprajñāta Samādhi, clear concentration associated with comprehension.*

By concentrating on this sound of the flute one realises that the same changes into the enchanting sound of the lute (Veenā Dhvani). With this achieved not only all doubts and confusion about the nature of the sound is dispelled, but one becomes filled with immense joy with the senses becoming submerged. This is the sign of achieving *Manipur Chakra*, the seat of *Vahnni Tattva*; the degree of concentration attained is named *Sānanda Samprajñāta Samādhi.*

With still deeper concentration the sound of the lute changes into one like the prolonged unbroken stream of sound of the gong (Ghantā Dhvani) which is called *Anāhata Nad*, when one is supposed to have entered the seat of *Vayu Tat-tva*—the *Anāhata Chakra* in the Shushumnā, *Bhima* of the Mahabharata. The name of the conch of Bhim is *Paundra*, the word being derived from 'Pandyante,' that which dispels. With the manifestation of this sound even the attributes of the heart are overcome. The degree of concentration achieved at this stage is called *Sasmitā Samprajnāta Samādhi*, when only a thin strain of one's existence, Asmita, remains.

The deepest and true concentration is achieved when the 'all conquering' sound of thunder or the sound of roar of the sea manifests. This is the sign of reaching the *Vishuddha* Chakra, the seat of *Vyoma Tattva*, in the region of the Shushumnā opposite the throat. At this stage all the attributes of the 'being' are overcome and *Asamprajnāta Samādhi* is attained. This stage of true concentration is represented as the eldest Pāndava, *Yudhishthir*.

The above five strains of sound next mingling together become audible as a cluster and has been called the Pānchajanya, the conch of Rishikesha, the 'lord of the senses.'

It may be recalled that aspirants after Yoga, almost invariably in every case, are seized with despondency at some early stage of his efforts when it is realised that further progress in higher stages of Yoga would require overcoming of all desires, good bad or indifferent, and suppression of the senses. Feeling of lethargy creeps in, and the aspirant gets inclined to slow down or stop performance of Yoga techniques. Such a state of mind is the most critical in the career of a Yogi. Loving and competent guidance of the preceptor or a very advanced incumbent in the path is essential at such a stage to get rid of this mental affliction. The message of the Gita provides such priceless guidance, which starts, in effect, from the Second Chapter, the Samkhya Yoga.

Sāmkhya Yoga

The notable instruction in the Sāmkhya Yoga is the direction to learn to distinguish between what is transient, perishable and destructible and what is permanent, imperishable and indestructible. All that appears, the different 'forms' or 'beings' and all experiences and suffering and happiness are transient; they come and go. But that which 'dwells' in every form or being is permanent and imperishable. When one dies it is his 'form' that changes and decays but not the 'Purusha' that dwells within the form. The Purusha—Chaitanya or Atma—the Self is not born, always exists and hence there can be no question of its death; the 'form,' *Deha*, however, in which the Chaitanya exists does change and die. Death is to be considered as a change of form just like change from birth to boyhood, youth and old age. The 'in dwelling' Purusha remains constant and unaffected. It is like changing an old and torn dress by the wearer and wearing of a new one. When the body—from wear and tear decays, the Spirit finds a new body. It is foolish to think that the 'in dweller', the soul, Atma or Purusha, can ever die. At the same time to think that what has been born will never die is another foolish-ness. Whatever is born is bound to die; it is unavoidable. As such one should not grieve over what is inevitable. Grief and despondency are unworthy traits and weakness of the heart, which should be shaken off.

After intellectual determination of the futility of grieving over the inevitable death and destruction of 'forms' of men and beings, and of the imperishability and indestructibility of the Self or Atma the advisability of adopting the path of *Buddhi Yoga* in the performance of efforts for Yoga has been emphasised. *Buddhi*, intelligence, is the manifestor of the Truth and is the divine instrument for correct comprehension. The greatest secret of getting rid of despondency is to establish oneself in the One-Pointed Buddhi and successfully discard the tentacles of desire, attachment and the ego, and thereby achieve Bliss, *Shanti* or Link with the Self, which is Yoga.

Karma Yoga

The Third Chapter titled the Karma Yoga constitutes the second lesson of the Gita. Towards the concluding part of the previous chapter effectiveness of Buddhi Yoga has been proclaimed, the one-pointed Buddhi, for those who mean business, and are determined to attain success. In this chapter which is devoted to exposition of the principles of Karma, work, lest there be confusion as to which path is preferred by the Gita, states at the outset that both the path of Jnāna, or intellectual determination and affirmation, and the path of Yoga or correct work—are of equal importance and efficacy. The moot point emphasised is that there are two kinds of attachment among men; for Jnāna Yoga by adherents of 'intellectual determination,' the Samkhyas, and of Karma Yoga by the Yogis. However, there is no basic difference in the results achieved; whatever can be achieved by the Sāmkhyas can also be attained by Yoga. The point stressed is that without performing any work or efforts one cannot achieve renunciation. Not only that, one cannot even survive without doing work! He cannot but work, in spite of himself, under the propulsion of the forces of the Prakriti—the Gunas. He has to learn, however, how purposefully he can perform work for fulfillment of his aim of reaching the goal of Yoga. The secret lies in knowing the art of doing work. The Gita says:

> "He excels who works with the organs only, by mentally controlling the subtle senses, without being attached; and that is Karma Yoga."*

*"Yastvindriyani Manasā Niyamyārabhatehrjuna Karmendriyaih Karma Yogam Ashakta Sa Visishyate." (3, 7)

To find out what is Karma, correct work, offers a confusing problem. The Gita declares that Karma has evolved from Brahma:

> "Know Karma as having evolved from Brahma, and Brahma from the Indestructible; Hence Brahma is all-pervasive, constantly established in holy work."**

> **"Karma Brahmodbhavam Viddhi Brahmākshara Samudbhavam Tasmāt Sarvagatam Brahma Nityam Yajne Pratishthitam." (3, 15)

The point is elaborated as to what is Karma in three other verses of this chapter:

> "Even the wise get perplexed to decide what is work and what is non-work. Hence I shall tell you what is work knowing which you will be freed from evil."***

> ***"Kim Karma Kim Akarmeti Kavayohpyatra Mohitāh Tattekarma Pravakshyāmi Yajjnātvā Mokshyasehsubhāt." (4, 16)

Again:

> "One should know what is Karma, what is Vikarma and what is Akarma; complex is the path of Karma."ā

> ā"Karmanohyapi Voddhavyam Voddhavyamcha Vikarmana Akarmanshcha Voddhvyam Gahanā Karmano Gatih." (4,17)

> "One who sees non-work (Akarma) in work and work in non-work he is the most intelligent among men; he is 'linked' in spite of doing all work."##

> ##"Karmanyakarma Yah Pasyetakarmani Cha Karma Yah Sa Buddhimān Manushyeshu Sah Yuktah Kritsnakarmakrit." (4, 18)

Work essentially is a direct concern of the organs of senses and of objects, which are subject to Gunas of Prakriti. What constitutes sin and causes bondage is not work as such but identification with the motive for work, resulting in generation of attachments and desires. In the words of the Gita:

> "This desire, this resentment (anger) borne out of Raja Guna, know them as the greatest sinners the most vicious enemies."###

> ###"Kāma Esha Krodha Esha Rajogunasamudbhavah Mahāshana Mahāpāpmā Viddhyenamiha Vairinam." (3,37)

It is clear, therefore, that the base of attachment, desires, lie in the senses, the mind and intelligence,—Indriyas, Manas and Buddhi;—attachment generated through these attributes shroud Jnāna and deludes the 'beings.' The relative position of these three base factors are:

> "Indriyas (organs of senses and action) are called superior, (That which is) superior to the Indriyas, is the mind;
>
> Superior to mind is Intelligence (Buddhi), and superior to the Buddhi is but He."*
>
> *"Indriyāni Parānyāhurindriebhyah Param Manah Manasastu Parā Buddhih Buddheryah Paratastu Sah." (3,42)

In another context, in chapter Eight to be precise, Karma has been defined as the 'evolver of ideas of beings,' and harps on the same refrains as verse 3-15 quoted above. Karma defined in the eighth chapter, reads:

> "Param Brahma is the Indestructible, His nature is Adhyātma, Generator of idea of beings is Visarga (Nada, Pranava) which is called Karma."**
>
> **"Akshara Paramam Brahma Svabhāvohdhyātmamuchyate Bhutabhāvodbhavakarah Visargah Karma Samjnita." (8, 3)

Jnana Yoga

The Fourth Chapter, named Jnana Yoga, deals with subtle attributes of the Spirit that are supposed to be involved in the make up of the human body; also have been described in this chapter, what is commonly believed to be, scriptural authentication of the principle of Divine Incarnation, Avatar-hood. Principles of occurrence of the Yugas and manifestation and withdrawal of the creative scenes, has also been laid down in this chapter. 'Jnana,' specifying the title of this chapter, has been defined as follows in the Gita later:

> "Also consider Me as the knower of the Field, Oh. descendant of Bharat in every Field; That which is *'knowing the Field and Knower of the Field'* is *Jnana*, is My view."*
>
> *"Kshetrajnamchapi Mām Viddhi Sarvakshetreshu Bhārata Kshetra Kshetrajnāyorjnānam Yattajjnānam Matam Mama." (XIII, 3)

This chapter contains one of the famous, what are known as, puzzles of Vyasa, the Vyasa-Kut, in its very first verses. In essence, however, these verses describe the 'link of the 'Spirit' in the human body. The texts read:

> "This imperishable Yoga I told the Sun (Vivasvan). The Sun told Manu (The original Father of man; "Manava", meaning man, has been derived from

Manu) and Manu told Ikshvaku (Ikshvaku = The name of the first King of
the solar dynasty, Surya Vansha);"

"In this way handed down from generation to generation Rajarshis came to
know it; that Yoga (link) during great efflux of time decayed."**

**"Imam Vivasvate Yogam Proktavānahamavyayam Vivasvān Manave Prāha
Manuriksvākavehvravit" "Evam Paramparāpraptamimam Rajarshayo Viduh
Sa Kālenehmahatā Yogo Nashtah Parantapah." (IV, 1&2)

The speaker of the above verses, Sree Krishna, says that he had first told the
Sun about this imperishable Yoga. The question naturally arises as to how
was this possible when the Sun had already existed when Sree Krishna was
born. The Gita of course gives its reply in its own style. Arjun asks:

"Your birth was posterior and that of the Sun anterior; How then could I
know that you told (the sun) first."***

***"Aparam Bhavato-Janma Vivasvatah Kathamaham Vijāniyam Tvamādau
Proktavāniti." (IV, 4)

The answer given by Shree Krishna is as under:

"Many births of mine and of yours have passed, Oh! Arjun; I am aware of all
of them, but you are not."#

#"Bahuni Me Vyatitāni Tava Chārjuna Tānyaham Vettha Na Tvam Vettah
Parantapa." (IV, 5)

The puzzle, Vyasa Kuta, referred to above are the two contentions, (i) how
was it possible for Shree Krishna, who was born much later, to have spoken
the Yoga to Vivasvan, the Sun, who came into existence long before; (ii) how
is it that the Yoga which was duly handed down from person to person could
have decayed or lost, which is against common human experience. When a
message or secret is duly handed down its preservation is rather ensured.

The first part of the contention has been attempted to be solved by
emphasising the conception of re-incarnation, of birth and re-birth as
contained in the quoted verse. The second part, that of the Yoga having been
lost even though it had been duly handed down the generations, from one
to the next is difficult to explain, in the normal run of human experience
and knowledge. The problem, however, can be solved logically by adopting
the Spiritual interpretation, which in the context of the back ground of the
story of the Maha Bharata and the Gita, as discussed in the foregoing, would
appear more plausible.

The various names involved in the above quoted verse after being analysed under spiritual interpretation would signify as follows:

Vivasvān is the sun which is considered as the repository of finer ingredients of creation in the solar system. The deep blue central part of the Sun is said to contain, in a condensed form, the ingredients which cause creation of the Universe. As such this part is said to be the Causal Body, Karana Sharira, of the universe. The dazzling aura around the deep blue central part is supposed to be the seat of 'Electrical' ingredients or Fine matters, Sukshma Bhutas, responsible for creation of Indriyas and Tanmatras, the subtle attributes; hence this dazzling part is known as the Sukshma Sharira, the Fine Material Body, of the universe. Conglomerates of the Fine Matters by permutation and combination produce the visible world, the Sthula Sharira of the universe. Of the sun moon and planets that constitute the universe, the sun represents the Karana Sharira, the moon the Sukshma Sharira and the planets the Sthula Sharira of the universal system. The different beings created in this universe including men also possess, being parts and parcels of the universe, the three phases of the above kind—the Causal, the Fine Material and the Gross Material. In the human body these three phases are said to be represented by the three principal Nadis—Ida, Pingala and Shushumna. They run from the lower part of the brain along the vertebral column to the Coccygeal region. Shushumna runs through the vertebral column, Pingala along its right side and Ida along the left. Pingala is known as the Surya Nadi, the seat of the Solar principle, Ida is called the Chandra Nadi—the seat of lunar principle and Shushumna is likened unto the heaven or Sky in the human body in which lie the planetary and stellar principles. Ida is known as the 'door' for contemplation or Dhyana by adopting which Chitta, the heart, gets tranquilled; Pingala is the 'door' for Jnana, true knowledge, of the subtle inner world. Ajnā Chakra on top of the Shushumnā, in between the eye-brows, is the seat of Kutastha Chaitanya which is seen by Kriya Yogis as a dense and deep blue shining circular ball surrounded by a brilliantly dazzling circular band of light. Just as the core the outer Sun is considered as the Causal Body of the Universe so is this deep blue region in the Ajna Chakra in respect of human body, wherein lies the Eternal Spirit—the Kutastha Chaitanya.

Manu: Manu is the progenitor of 'man,' Manava, whence idea of separateness begins. The white circular band of light encircling the afore-mentioned deep blue shining circular ball is considered to be the repository of fine materials and subtle objects constituting the Sukshma Sharira that are at the root of evolving fine material attributes of the human form.

Ikshvāku: He is the first king of Surya Vansha, Solar Dynasty, of the epic. It has been stated already that Nadis that arise out of Pingala constitute Surya Vansha. Pingala Nadi extends from Ajnā Chakra to the coccygeal region. The first point of contact of Pingala with the Ajnā Chakra is said to be the 'first king of the solar dynasty' who was named Ikshvaku.

Rājarshaya: The Rajarshis: Arshayan (collecting), Rājate (manifest);—centres of manifestations of the spirit,—the different astral Chakras within the Shushumna.

Although the Spirit is present everywhere and in every thing, as there can be nothing out side and without the Spirit, in the later stages of manifestation of the creative scenes awareness of this in beings Spirit becomes dim and virtually lost.

The two verses quoted above therefore do not propound any incongruity, but rather lay down the basic conceptions of subtle objects in the human body as taught by Hindu scriptures.

After laying down how the Spiritual 'link' is maintained in life, and how awareness of the 'link' gets lost or submerged, the Gita propounds the principles of the phenomenon of creation, of manifestation of the different 'forms.'

> "Even though I am without birth, and am of Indestructible Self, the Lord of the 'beings',"
>
> "Resting on My own nature I manifest through My own Maya."
>
> "Whenever Dharma is seized upon with lassitude and its opposite arises I create My Self."*
>
> *"Ajohpi Sannavyayātmā Bhutānāmisvarohpi San Prakritim Svamadhisthāya Sambhavāmyatmamāyayā."
>
> "Yadā Yadā Hi Dharmasya Glānirbhavati Bhārata Abhyuthhānamadharmasya Tadātmānam Srijāmyaham." (IV, 6 & 7)

The Dharma in the above context is the Spirit that always exists in the created 'beings' and 'holds' the creation; nothing can exist for a moment without the Spirit being present in it. In the words of Lord Gouranga Jiva, the being, is but a Spirit-Matter knot, Chit-Jada Granthi. The Spirit and Prakriti in all its deformation being 'entangled' together cause appearance of the being.

Referring to the Samkhya postulates of Kapil it has already been described how by deformations (Vikriti) of Prakriti, which is but a Nature of the Divinity, in the presence of the Spirit the scheme of creation becomes possible. Prakriti has been defined as:

"State of equilibrium of Sattva, Raja and Tama (Gunas)."**

**"Sattva Raja Tamasām Sāmyavasthā Prakitiryādi." (Kanāda Sutras: 1, 61)

Disequilibrium of the three Gunas constituting Prakriti is the prime cause of creation, and is the effect of the divine Maya generating ideas of division and of plurality in the Absolute and the Unity. In what process and why this is done has been hinted in the very next verse.

"For saving the pious and destroying the sinful and for establishing *Dharma* I manifest (Myself) in Yugas and Yugas."***

"Paritrānāya Sādhunām Vināshāya Sambhavāmi mi uge Yuge." (IV, 8)

In the chapter on the Yuga that follows this subject has been discussed in some details. Appearance and disappearance of different Yugas, referred to as Day-Night (Aho-Ratra) and of Kalpa are essential features in the nature of things, and may at best be described as the Divine Game, the Lila. Characteristics of different Yugas are manifestations or otherwise of certain inner virtues. Similar virtues are capable of being developed in an individual also by performing the 'Yuga' technique or Yugala Mantra, which is Kriya or Pranayama. These two verses are frequently quoted as scriptural authority for the popularly held idea of Incarnation of God, Avatarvad. That such ideas are not what the Gita teaches can be appreciated from the very nature of things as described in the texts. When nothing can be conceived of as outside the Divinity how and where can the Lord descend! The verses depict on the other hand the basic Hindu conception of creation, of evolution and devolution of the universal picture under the Divine Play of Maya. The verse that follows is more significant in this respect.

"He who knows these My resplendent and secret birth and work does not go to birth again but goes to Me."*

*"Janma Karma Cha Me Divyamevam Yo Vetti Tattvatah Tyaktva Deham Punarjanma Naiti Māmeti Sohrjuna." (IV, 9)

The points to emphasise from this observation are, (i) birth and work referred to are not ordinary affairs, but Divine (Divyam); (ii) these birth and work can be 'known' by men but in their 'essence' only and (iii) the one who can know these can escape the labyrinthine chain of births and re-births and may even attain Him. It is evident therefore that the verses quoted are in conformity only with the basic conceptions of the message of the Gita.

Discussion in this chapter then logically flows into determining what is correct work or efforts that could re-establish the 'link' with the Spirit and ultimately can bring about attainment of Kaivalya, One-ness with the Divinity. Verses have been laid down there-after in this chapter detailing types of correct 'Karma'. The secret of correct Karma, according to the Gita, is forsaking desires for fruits of work or labour, and maintaining an attitude of contentment all the while.

> "Forsaking attachment for fruits of labour even if one engages in work being always contented within and unattached, he does not 'do' any work."*

> *"Tyaktva Karmaphalāsangam Nityatripto Nirāsrayah Karmānyābhi pravrit-tohpi Naiva Kinchit Karoti Sah." (IV, 20)

Works that are conducive to generating the above condition of mind or tendencies have been called Yajna, holy work; and many kinds of Yajnas have been mentioned. While describing various types of holy work principles of Pranayama have also been narrated.

> "Performers of Pranayama sacrifice out-going breath into the in-coming and the in-coming into the out-going thereby stopping the flow of Prana and Apana."**

> **"Apāne Yuhvati Prānam Prānehpānam Tathāpare Prānāpānagatiruddhā Prānāyāmaparāyanh." (IV, 29)

The above description of Pranayama in fact outlines the technique as practised by adherents of Kriya Yoga. In the following verse Jnāna Yajna which is the result of Kriya Yoga has been eulogised as the best of all types of holy work.

> "Jnana Yajna is better than holy work involving material sacrifice, as all holy work in the long run ends in Jnāna. And the 'fire of Jnāna' burns all work linked with desire to ashes in the same way as sacrificial fire does the fire wood."***

> ***"Sreyan DravyamāyadyajnādJnāna Yajna Parantapa Sarvam Karmākhilam Pārtha Jnāne Parisamāpyate." (IV, 33)

This Jnāna, it has been emphasised, has to be received directly from an actual 'knower,' from a Guru.

> "You will be 'advised' of this Jnāna by one that is a 'knower' of the Principles or Tattvas; You have to learn it through reverence, questioning and service."*

*"Tadviddhi Pranipātena Pariprasnena Seveyā Upadekshyanti Te Jnāninastat-tvadarsinah." (IV, 34)

The age old tradition in matters of spiritual culture is that initiation, Upadesh, has got to be in the direct line from the teacher to the disciple in an unbroken chain. The Gita has naturally emphasised this traditional concept.

Saint Tulsidas's couplet in this context has the same refrain as the above verse of the Gita.

> "When you get a true teacher (Sad Guru) who shows the secret by imparting Jnāna; It is likened unto dark colour of coal being dispelled when fire enters into it."**

> **"Sad Guru Paove Bhed Vataove Jnānkar Upadesh Tav Koilake Maila Chhute Jav Ag Karaye Pravesh."

Enshrined in the above verse is the age-old concept of the importance of the Guru in the life of a spiritual aspirant.

The stirring call of the Gita to any Yoga aspirant afflicted by dejection and despondency has been embodied in the following verse.

> "Hence tearing off this doubt of the heart arising out of ignorance, with your sabre of Jnāna and raising yourself remain in Yoga."***

> ***"Tasmād Ajnānasambhutam Hritstham Jnānāsinātmanah Chhithvainam Samshayam Yogamātishtothhishtha Bhārata." (IV, 42)

Sannyāsa Yoga

Emphasis laid in the previous chapter on Jnāna, true knowledge, and perfor-mance of work without attachment for fruits of work raises the question of renunciation, Sannyās—renunciation of fruits or results of performance. The question is what has been advocated for adoption? whether it is advised that one should practise no work or engage in doing Karma. In this chapter the Gita advises the distinction and relation between the two concepts:

> "Both renunciation and Yoga are capable of causing supreme excellence; But of the two, Karma Yoga is superior to renunciation of work."*

> *"Sannyāsah Karmayogascha Nihsreyashakaravubhau Tayostu Kar-masannyāsāt Karmayogo Visishyate." (V, 2)

The above verse affirms that although in essence both the paths end ultimately in similar achievements, adoption of only mental processes is not advocated.

In the fourth and fifth verses processes of mental contemplation, as envisaged in the Samkhya path has been compared with Yoga. The secret, however, has been described in the tenth verse.

"Children and not the wise say that Samkhya and Yoga are different; Completely possessed of one gives the fruits of both."

"Whatever is achievable by Samkhya can also be achieved by Yoga; He sees correctly who sees both Samkhya and Yoga as equal."**

**"Sāmkyayogau Prithagvālā Pravadanti Na Panditah Ekamapyāsthitah Samyagubhayourvindate Phalam." "Yat Sāmkhyairprāpyate Sthānam Tat Yogairapi Gamyate Ekam Sāmkhyam Cha Yogam Cha Ya Pasyati Sa Pasyati." (V, 4&5)

The secret, however, lies in performing work under proper discipline, as stated below:

"Surrendering all resolve for work in Brahma, if one performs work by forsaking attachments, He does not get implicated in sin, like the lotus leaf (plunged) in water."***

***"Brahmanyādhāya Karmāni Sangam Tyaktvā Karoti Yah Lipyate Na Sa Pāpena Padmapatramivāmbhasā." (V, 10)

Expanding the edict more clearly in the next verse, the Gita declares:

"The Yogis perform work by the body, mind, intelligence and the Indriyas (organs of senses and actions) only but severing attachments with their objects, for the purification of Self."#

#"Kāyena Manasā Buddhy Samnyasyāste Sukham Vasi Kevalairindriyairapi Yoginah Karma Kurvanti Sangam Tyaktvā Atmasuddhaye." (V, 11)

The theme is further elaborated in the following:

"Mentally renouncing all functions (of Indriyas) the In-Dweller remains calm and poise within the nine-doored city without working nor causing work."##

##"Sarvakarmāni Manasā Samnyasyāste Sukham Vasi Navadvāre Pure Dehi Naiva Kurvan Na Kārayan." (V, 13)

The human body is referred to as the nine-door city, counting its nine openings: the two eyes, two ears, two nostrils, the mouth, the generative organ and the anus. The Yogi who gets established in his Self is unaffected by the actions of the senses and attributes of Chitta and of delusion and ignorance.

The Gita affirms that basically the Lord has made his created beings free of all encumbrances.

> "The Lord does not create for beings mastery, nor work neither link with result of work; they are caused under Svabhāva, the nature-Prakriti."*

> "The Lord does not accept sin nor virtue of any being: the living beings are deluded because (their) Jnāna is enveloped by Ajnāna."**

> *"Na Kartritvam Na Karmāni Lokasya Srijati Prabhu Na Karmaphalasamyo-gam Svabhāvastu Pravartate." (V, 14)

> **"Nādatte Kasyachit Pāpam Na Chaiva Sukritam Vibhuh Ajnānenāvritam Jnānam Tena Muhyanti Jantavah." (V, 15)

Among the methods advocated to get rid of the above mentioned implications of senses, attributes of Chitta and of delusion the following all-time significant instructions have been laid down:

> "The sage who aspiring after salvation controls the Indriyas, mind and intelligence by keeping out external objects concentrating the eyes in between the eyebrows within and harmonising the breaths within the nostrils and whose desire, fear and anger are gone he is always free."***

> ***"Sparshān Kritvā Vahirvāhyaschakshuschaivāntare Bhruvoh Prānāpānau Same Kritvā Nāsābhyantarachārinau." "Yatendriyamanobuddhirmunirmok shaparāyanah Vigatechchābhayakrodho Ya Sada Mukta Eva Sah." (V, 27 & 28)

Abhyāsa or Dhyāna Yoga

After discussing Sāmkhya, Karma, Jnāna and Sannyāsa Yoga in the second, third, fourth and fifth chapters,—which have been seen as complementary and interdependent the Gita in the sixth chapter describes in detail the practical application of Yoga. As such it has been aptly designated as Abhyāsa Yoga. The very first verse describes what kind of Abhyasa or Practice has been advocated. The verse reads:

> "He who performs abandoning all attachment to the result thereof as duty, Is a Sannyasi as well as a Yogi; but not he who refrains from action as a ritual."*

> *"Anāsrita Karmaphalam Kāryam Karma Karoti Yah Sa Sannyasi Cha Yogi Cha Na Niragnirnachākriya. (VI, 1)

The same theme has been further emphasised in the next verse.

"What is called Sannyasa, know that oh! son of Pandu, as Yoga; No one can ever be a Yogi without abandoning resolve for work."**

**"Yam Sannyāsamiti Prāhuryogam Tam Viddhi Pāndava Na Hyasan-yastasamkalpo Yogi Bhavati Kaschana." (VI, 2)

After detailing how a Yogi acts, behaves and feels, the Gita then lays down the methods of performances for attaining Yoga. In fact the twenty two verses of this chapter beginning with the eleventh may be said to be out and out Yoga instructions. These are so straight forward that they do not need much elaboration and may as well be quoted straight.

"Establishing a firm seat for self at a pure and clean place, neither high nor low, placing Kusha grass, antelope skin and linen one above the other; There taking his seat one should practice Yoga for purification of self by making the mind one-pointed and controlling the functions of the heart and the senses."***

***"Suchau Deshe Pratishthāpya Sthirāmasānamātmanah Nātyuchhritam Nātinicham Chailājinakusottaram;" "Tatraikāgram Manah Kritvā Yatachitte ndriyakriyāhUpāvisyāsane Yunjyād Yogamātmavisuddhaye." (VI, 11 & 12)

Selection of a suitable place for practising Yoga is important. Directions of the Gita in this respect as given above, have to be considered in their proper perspective. Swami Sri Yukteshvar used to say that in the times of the Gita when Rishis and sages used to live in huts and leaf cottages in forests, care had to be taken to ensure that seat for spiritual performances had been properly insulated against dampness and electricity. Directions contained in the above verse were meant to ensure the above requirements. In modern times, however, when people normally lived in bricked houses and dry places, a piece of blanket covered with some soft material like linen may serve as a good seat; and the place may as well be a room kept clean and provided with door and windows for proper ventilation. The door and window may be closed from within to cut off disturbing noises and direct blasts of air.

The next Sloka shows in what posture should one sit on the above seat.

"By holding immovably and steady the body, head and neck in a line and gaz-ing at the root of the nose without looking at the sides;" "He should be calm, fearless, determined in the pursuit of the divine and with the mind controlled and engaged in surrendering in Me."ā

#"Samam Kāya Sirogrivam Dhārayanachalam Sthirah Samprekshya Nāsikāgram Svam Disaschānavalokayan;" "Prasāntātmā Vigatabhirbrahmachārivrate Sthirah Manah Samyamya Macchitto Yukta Asita Matpara." (VI, 13 & 14)

The above edict, although looks concise and brief, in actuality includes the relevant instructions as contained in the Sadhan Pad of Pātanjal Yoga Sutras; of observing Yama Niyama, Asana, Pranayama, Pratyahara, Dharana, Dhyana and Samadhi to equip one self with requisite capacities to 'surrender' to Him, for becoming 'Matpara.' The resultant effect is described as follows:

"The Yogi who in this way always controls the mind attains Supreme Bliss that abides in Me."##

##"Yunjannevam Sadātmānam Yogi Niyata Mānasah Santim Nirvānaparamam Matsansthāmadhigachchhati." (VI, 15)

Instructions on Yoga have been so thorough that even how a Yogi should otherwise lead his life has not been overlooked. Thus:

"Yoga is not for one who eats too much, nor who abstains (from food) too much; neither for him who is too much addicted to sleep or too much wakefulness."

"One who is regulated in his food and living, regulated in work and efforts and regulated in sleep and wakefulness, for him Yoga becomes the killer of sufferings."###

###"Nātyasnatastu Yogohsti Na Chaikāntamanasnata Na Chātisvapnasilashya Jāgrato Naiva Chārjuna;" "Yuktāhāravihārasya Yuktachestasya Karmashu Yuktasvapnavavodhasya Yogo Bhavati Duhkhahā" (VI, 16 & 17)

Different stages and conditions of the Yogi have next been described:

"He whose heart is fully harmonised and who remains absorbed in Self and who is free from all kinds of longings is said to be in tune or in link."*

*"Yadā Viniyatam Chittamātmanyevavatisthate Nisprihah Sarvakāmebhyo Yukta Ityuchyate Tadā." (VI, 18)

"He remains absorbed in Yoga unruffled and is likened unto the lamp in a place without wind and burns without flickers."**

**"Yathā Dipo Nivātastho Nengate Sopamā Smritā Yogino Yatachittasaya Yunjato Yogamātmanah." (VI, 19)

"When by practice of Yoga the mind is rested and is satisfied at being face to face with the Spirit."***

***"Yatroparamate Chittam Niruddham Yogasevayā Yatra Chaivātmanātmānam Pasyannātmani Tushyati." (VI, 20)

"He enjoys endless delight which can be grasped by Buddhi (intelligence) but beyond the ken of the senses; and being settled in that stage does not deflect from that."#

#"Sukhamātyantikam   Yattabuddhigrāhyamatindriyam   Vetti   Yatra   Na Chaivāyam Sthitaschalati Tattvatah." (VI, 21)

"Having achieved that than which, he felt, there was no greater gain outside it, and established in which even grave sorrows cannot disturb him."##

##"Yam Lavdhvā Chāparam Lābham Manyate Nādhikam Tatah Yasmin Shito Na Duhkhena Gurunāpi Vichālyate." (VI, 22)

"That should be k nown   as   Yoga,   which   is   separation   from   pain; and he should practise this Yoga with firm determination and without despondence."###

###"Tam Vidyāddukhasamyogaviyogam Yogasamjnitam Sa Nischayena Yoktavyo Yogohnirvinnachetasā." (VI, 23)

"By completely abandoning all propensities that beget desires and mentally curbing all senses;"*

*"Samkalpa PrabhavānKāmāmstyaktvā Svarānaseshatah Manasaivendriyagrāmam Viniyamya Samantatah;" (VI, 24)

"He should slowly and slowly withdraw by directing the mind within self and without thinking of anything else;"**

**"Sanaih Sanairuparamed Buddhyā Dhritigrihitayā Atmasamstham Manah Kritvā Na Kinchidapi Chintayet;" (VI, 25)

"As often as the mind wavers, becomes unsteady and runs away, so often it should be checked and brought under control."***

***"Yato Yato Nishchalati Manaschanchalamasthiram Tatastato Niyamyai Tadāmanyeva Vasam Nayet." (VI, 26)

"A Yogi of this calibre who is mentally poised and who has calmed his propensities, achieves the highest taintless joy of Brahma."ā

#"Prasāntamanasam Hyenam Yoginām Sukhamuttamam Upaiti Santarajasam Brahmabhutamakalmasham." (VI, 27)

"By practising Yoga in this way the Yogi becomes taintless and achieves contacts with the Brahma and enjoys Infinite Bliss."##

##"Yunjannevam Sadātmānam Yogi Vigatakalmashah Sukhena Brahmasamsparsamatyantam Sukhamasnute." (VI, 28)

"Poised in Yoga he comprehends the Spirit (Atma) in all beings and all beings in the Spirit and perceives the same everywhere."###

###"Sarvabhutasthamātmānam Sarva Bhutāni Chātmani Ikshate Yog-ayuktātmā Sarvatrasamadarsana." (VI, 29)

When a Yogi achieves the above stage of development he is guaranteed the following divine assurance:

"He who comprehends Me in every thing and every thing in Me, him I shall never lose hold of, nor shall he lose hold of Me."*

*"Yo Mām Pasyanti Sarvatra Sarvamcha Mayi Pasyati Tasyāham Na Pra-nasyāmi Sa Cha Me Na Paranasyati." (VI, 30)

"He who worships Me as the Unity abiding in all beings, whichever manner he may live, that Yogi lives in Me."**

**"Sarvabhutasthitam   Yo   Mām   Bhajatyekatvamāsthitah   Sarvathā Vartamānohpi Sa Yogi Mayi Vartate." (VI, 31)

"He who, in the same way as the Spirit, sees the same in every thing whether pleasant or painful is considered a perfect Yogi."***

***"Atmoupamyena Sarvatra Samam Pasyati Yohrjuna Sukham Vā Dukham Sa Yogi Paramo Matah." (VI, 32)

A more eloquent and precise lesson on Yoga is inconceivable. It is comprehensive and all facts of the career of a Yogi has been duly taken cognisance of and necessary instructions left. Two other questions that often arise in the minds of aspirants after Yoga have also been dealt with in this chapter. One is the question that is frequently faced by every Yoga-aspirant relating to the problem of controlling the mind. Arjun asks:

"Oh, Krishna the mind is restless, erring, strong and rigid; I consider control-ling this extremely difficult like controlling the breaths."ā

#"Chanchalam Hi Manah Krishna Pramāthi Balavaddridham Tasyāham Nigraham Manye Vāyoriva Sudushkaram." (VI, 34)

The answer given by the Lord is at the same time logical and practical.

"Doubtless, Oh great warrior the mind is restless and very difficult to control; but this can be controlled by perseverance and by detachment."##

##"Asamsayam Mahāvāho Mano Durnigraham Chalam Abhyāsena Ty Kaun-teya Vairāgyena Cha Grihyate." (VI, 35)

Solution offered by the Yoga Sutras in this respect is identical:

"That can be curbed by continuous practice and by indifference."###
###"Abhyāsa Vairāgyabhyām Tannirodhah." (Samadhi pad, 12)

Abhyasa again has been defined as:

"Dedicated efforts to remain in the state aimed at is Abhyasa."

"Abhyasa is consolidated through prolonged, regular without break and devoted practice."*

*"Tatra Sthitau Yatnobhyāsa." (Samadhi Pad, 13)

"Sa Tu Dirghakāla Nairantarya Satkāra Sevito Dridhabhumi." (Samadhi Pad, 14)

Vairagya has been defined as:

"Indifference generated to objects seen and heard called the controlled state—Vashikar—is Vairagya."**

**"Drishtānushravikavishayavitrishnāvashikara Samjna Vairāgyam." (Samadhi Pad, 15)

The answer to the first question, therefore, is observance of repeated practice and inculcation of indifference—Abhyasa and Vairagya.

The second question relates to what happens if after taking up practice of Yoga the Yogi ultimately does not pursue it to its logical end; in that case will all cares and devotion with which practice of Yoga was undertaken come to a total naught if the practice is given up midway? The answer given is not only re-assuring but consists of one of the basic conceptions of the Hindu spiritual culture.

"Oh Partha neither in this life nor in the life to come is there destruction for him; never does any who works righteousness tread the path of woe."***

***"Pārtha Naiveha Nāmutra Vināsastasya Vidyate Nahi Kalyānakrit Kaschiddurgatim Tāta Gacchati." (VI, 40)

"He who falls from Yoga is re-born in a pure and virtuous household. Or he may even be born in a family of Yogis; such a re-birth is most rare in this world."ā

#"Suchinām Srimatām Gehe Yogabrashta Abhijāyate." "Athavā Yogināmeva Kule Bhavati Dhimatām Etaddhi Durlabhataram Loke Janma Yadidrisham." (VI, 41 & 42)

The assurance does not end here, but extends further:

"There he receives the characteristics (Buddhi Yoga) attained in the former body; and with these he again labours for perfection. He is irresistibly swept away by that former habit, and seeking Yoga goes above the Word of Brahma (Pranava)."##

##"Tatra Tam Buddhi Samyogam Labhate Purvadaihikam Yatate Cha Tato Bhuiyo Samsiddhau Kurunandana." "Purvābhyāsena Tenaiva Kriyate Hyavashohpi Sah Jijnāsurapi Yogasya Savdabrahmātivartate." (VI, 43 & 44)

In this way by assiduously performing Yoga one becomes purified, through many births, of the accumulated dross and attains complete emancipation which is the supreme goal. As such, in this chapter the Gita has hailed Yoga as the best path and the Yogi as the best among performers of spiritual efforts.

"The Yogi is greater than the ascetic; he is also considered greater than the wise (Jnani); the Yogi is also greater than men of action; therefore become a Yogi. Among all the Yogis again one that devotedly worships Me by being immersed inwardly with My Atma is considered by Me to be the best."###

###"Tapasvibhyohdhikoyogi Jnānibhyohpi Matohdhika Karmibhy-aschādhikoyogi Tasmādyogi Bhavārjuna;" "Yogināmapi Sarveshām Madgatenāntarātmanā Sraddhāvan Bhajate Yo Mām Sa Me Yuktatamo Matah." (VI, 46 & 47)

Vijnana Yoga

After thus laying down practical aspects of Yoga, the Gita in the seventh chapter deals with Vijnana Yoga or 'Comprehensive knowledge.' All postulates that have been discussed in the introductory part of this treatise can be found elaborated in this chapter. It lays down that there are two kinds of Nature, Prakriti, of the Divine:

"Earth, Water, Fire, Air, Vacuum (Vyoma) and Mind, Intelligence and Ego constitute My separate (Inferior) eight-fold nature, Prakriti."*

*"Bhumirāponala Vāyuh Khang Manubuddhireva Cha Ahamkāra Itiyam Me Bhinnā Prakritirashtadhā." (VII, 4)

The above affirmation, it will be found, is identical with the Samkhya edict on creation. Another Nature of the Divine is then described.

"There is another Nature of Mine, which is the Superior—the Para Prakriti—which becoming 'beings' upholds the running of universal scene."**

**"Apareyamitastvanyam Prakritim Viddhi Me Parām Jivabhutam Mahāvāho Yayedam Dhāryate Jagat." (VII, 5)

Creation is the outcome of these two Nature of the Divine; and thus in the ultimate analysis it is the Divinity that is at the root of creation and destruction of the Apparent Universe.

> "From out of this 'womb' have evolved all the beings and are held together; I am the cause of creation as well as destruction of everything in the World."***

> ***"Etadyonini Bhutāni Sarvānityupadhāraya Aham Kritsnasya Jagatah Prabhavah Pralayastatha." (VII, 6)

> "There is nothing whatsoever which is greater than Me; all these apparent are woven in Me like jewels woven into the lace."ā

> #"Mattah Parataram Nānyat Kinchidasti Dhananjaya Mayi Sarvamidam Protam Sutre Maniganā Iva." (VII, 7)

In all the subsequent verses the principal theme has been elaboration of the above principles. It is the Spirit that is the Essence of all that exists, the seed and the vital feature. Thus:

> "I am the eternal seed of all beings, Intelligence of the wise and energy of the energetic;"##

> ##"Vijam Mām Sarvabhutānām Viddhi Pārtha Sanātanam Buddhirbuddhimatāmasmi Tejastejasvinamaham." (VII, 10)

All the beings, the created, are products of the three Gunas which have kept them bewildered; hence the created cannot comprehend the Indestructible, the Real Cause, the Supreme Spirit. The products under the Divine Maya, Delusion, are innumerable and vast, but can only be overcome by 'worshipping' the Divine.

The devotees that are engaged in the above 'worship' are of four types:

> "Four types of virtuous beings worship Me; the afflicted, the inquisitive, the ones seeking wealth and the wise. Amongst them the constantly 'linked' wise with one-pointed devotion is the best; even as I am the object of love of the Jnani, so is he dear to Me."###

> ###"Chaturvidhā Bhajante Mām Janāh Sukritinohrjuna Artto Jijnāshurarthārthi Jnānicha Bharatarshava."

> "TeshāmJnāni Nityayukta Ekabhaktirvisishyate Priyohi Jnāninohtyarthamaham Sa Cha Mama Priya." (VII, 16 & 17)

Akshar Brahma Yoga

In the eighth chapter, the Akshar Brahma and Its different aspects in different stages of creation, distinction between the Indestructible and other states, have been shown as under:

> The Indestructible is the Supreme Eternal—Param Brahma; His essential Nature is Adhyatma; the Visarga—the Omkara—that causes evolution of ideas of beings is called Karma. His Nature in the perishable beings is Adhibhuta; that which dwells in form (Purusha) is Adhidaiva and that which is present in all the forms of all the holders of body or form is Me, is called the Adhi Yajna.*

> *"Akshara Paramam Brahma Svabhyāvohdhyātmamuchyate Bhutabhāvodbhavakarovisargah Karmasamjnitah" "Adhibhutam Ksharobhāvah Puruscha Adhidaivatam Adhiyajnamahamevātra Dehe Dehabhritam Varah." (VIII, 3 & 4)

Definition of Adhi Yajna here is significant; the pronoun "I" (Aham) in this connection stands for the speaker of the Gita, Sree Krishna. It is also synonymous with Kutastha Chaitanya.

In the fifth, twelfth and the thirteenth verses of the chapter the Gita has taught how to cast off one's body, how to die, so as not to suffer re-birth again. Everything in the Universe is subject to 'coming and going,' of birth and death, and this cycle ceases only when one reaches Him.

> "All the beings in the universe, including Brahma, are subject to (the law of) coming again and again; but once reaching Me, the Divine, there is no further re-birth."**

> **"Abrahmabhuvanālokāh Punarāvartinohrjuna Māmupetya Tu Kāunteya Punarjanma Na Vidyate." (VIII, 16)

That Brahma is also a 'being'—the Great Being—and subject to births—has been emphasised in the next verse:

> "They are the knowers of Day-Night, Aho-Ratra, who know that one thousand Yugas constitute a Day of Brahma and one thousand Yugas His Night."***

> ***"Sahasrayugaparyantamaharyadbrahmanoviduh Rātrim Yugasahasrāntam Te Ahorātravidojanah." (VIII, 17)

It will be seen in the chapter on the Yuga that Yugas, in the above quoted verse, is the Daiva Yuga. All changes that follow is a continuous sequence of 'appearance' and 'disappearance' and described as Aho-Ratra in Hindu scriptural representations, which follow the Universal processes. Appearance and disappearance is a feature in this process, in a chain of sequences, which is the inexorable law of nature. The Gita says:

> "All things are manifested from out of Avyakta, Prakriti, with the advent of the Day; with the approach of Night they dissolve into that Prakriti again."ā

> #"Avyaktādvyaktayah Sarvāh Prabhavantyaharāgame Ratryāgame Praliyante Tatraivāvyaktasamjnake." (VIII, 18)

> "All these beings appear and disappear again and again automically of their own; at the approach of Night they disappear to reappear again with the advent of the Day."##

> ##"Bhutagrāmah Sa Evāyam Bhutvā Bhutvā Praliyate Rātryāgamehvāsah Pārtha Prabhavatyaharāgame." (VIII, 19)

> "The Superior Nature which is (un-manifest) and higher than the above Avyakta is the Ever-Existent, and which is not destroyed even when all the beings are destroyed."###

> ###"Paratasmāttu Bhāvohnyahvyaktohvyaktāt Sanātanah Yah Sarveshu Bhuteshu Nāsyatsu Na Vināshyati." (VIII, 20)

According to the fore-going everything in the universal picture is subject to a sequence of appearance and disappearance, from out of the unmanifest Avyakta under its own inexorable laws and back to Avyakta again. There is, however, the superior Indestructible and the Ever-Existent which is above the laws of the Unmanifest, the Prakriti.

Raja Guhya Yoga

The Ninth Chapter, designated as the Raja Guhya Yoga, is but an extension of the topics of discussion in the Eighth Chapter. All the beings are created by the Prakriti, which is the Divine Nature; the Divinity—the Spirit—having been the ultimate cause for their creation. Every thing is 'lodged' in Him; nothing can be conceived of as outside the Divine.

> "Like the excellent air which moves about in the sky everywhere, all beings have their stay in Me;"*

> *"Yathākāshasthito Nityam Vāyuh Sarvatrago Mahān Tahtā Sarvāni Bhutāni Matsthānityupādhāraya." (IX, 6)

> "All the beings Oh, son of Kunti! enter My Prakriti at the conclusion of the Kalpa (a Day of Brahma); they are created by Me again at the beginning of the Kalpa (the Kalpa that follows)."**

**"Sarvabhutāni Kaunteya Prakritim Yānti Māmikām Kalpakshaye Punastāni Kalpādau Visrijamyaham." (IX, 7)

The next verse has the same refrain as when the principle of 'link' of the Spirit has been described in the Fourth Chapter.

"Settled in My own Prakriti I create all those clusters of beings through the nature of Prakriti, again and again without will or desire."***

***"Prakritim Svāmavashtabhya Visrijāmi Punah Punah Bhutagrāmamimam Kritsnamavasham Prakritervāshat." (IX, 8)

There is no distinction of birth and caste in one's abilities to progress along the path of spiritual attainments; the most important perquisite is 'one-pointed' devotion—Eko Bhakti. Spiritual efforts are devoted to 'cleansing' of the dross, of the sins, accumulated over the years and births, which may extend over several births. There is no question whether one is a more or a less sinner or virtuous; one-pointed devotion even by the worst sinner may make him a recognised saint.

'I am the Goal, the Sustainer, the Lord, the witness, the Shelter, the Refuge, the Companion, the Root, the End, the Existence, the Base and the Imperishable Seed.'ā

#"Gatirbhartā Prabhuh Sākshi Nivāsa Saranam Suhrit Prabhavah Pralayah Sthānam Nidhānam Vijamavyayam." (IX, 18)

Whoever can establish himself in the above devotion can attain the goal, including the worst sinner.

'Even if the most wicked amongst the wicked surrenders in Me with one-pointed devotion he should be considered a saint, as he has completely reconciled and succeeded in his efforts.'##

"Apichet Sudurāchāro Bhajate MāmananyabhākSādhureva Samantavya Samyagvyavashito Hi Sa." (IX, 30)

Swami Sri Yukteshvar held that the principal message of the Gita can be obtained from its first nine chapters. When his Spiritual Interpretations were first published these were limited to the first nine chapters only. However, the Swami kept brief notes on the remaining nine chapters, evidently made from talks of Shri Shri Lahiri Mahasaya, which were preserved in the Swami's safe. After his demise in 1936 the present author discovered them wrapped in a linen and kept in a corner of the iron safe. The second edition of this holy book published by Sevayatan Ashram, Jhargram, in 1948 incorporated these notes also.

It has been already mentioned that according to Swami Sri Yukteshvar the last nine chapters of the Gita contained elaborations and explanations of the themes already laid down in the first nine chapters.

Vibhuti Yoga

The Tenth Chapter is called the *Vibhuti Yoga*, or the Yoga of Special Manifestations or Revelations. In the words of Lord Sree Krishna He is that which appears as special in every class of creation; He is the King among men, Himalaya among the mountains and so on.

Vishvarup Darsana Yoga

Vishvarup Darsana Yoga is the Eleventh Chapter of the holy book. It gives a description of spiritual experiences of super-natural magnitude; these experiences can be induced in a devoted advanced disciple by a competent Spiritual Master. Experience of similar nature was induced in Swami Vivekananda by Sri Sri Ramkrishna Paramhansa. Paramhansa Yogananda also narrated similar experiences induced in him by Sri M, the biographer of Sri Ramkrishna as well as by his Guru Swami Sri Yukteshvar.

Bhakti Yoga

The Twelfth Chapter is designated as the *Bhakti Yoga*, the Yoga of Devotion. **Prakriti Purusha Vibhāga Yoga or Kshetra-Kshetrajna Vibhāga Yoga** is the name given to the Thirteenth Chapter. Both the names, as has been shown earlier, give the same meaning. Kshetra is equivalent to Prakriti with its attributes and Kshetrajna—the knower of Kshetra—is the Purusha. Reference has been made to the definition of Kshetra when interpreting Dharma Kshetra and Kuru Kshetra. Knowing of the essence and the difference between the Kshetra and the Kshetrajna constitutes Jnana.

The Fourteenth Chapter named *Guna Traya Vibhaga Yoga* lays down different definitions of the three Gunas—Sattva, Raja and Tama. To quote:

> 'The Sattva being taintless is manifester of that which is free from suffering, but which 'binds through happiness and cognition.'*

> *"Tatra Satvam Nirmalatvāt Prakāsakamanāmayam Sukhasangena Vadhnāti Jnānasangena Chānagha." (XIV, 6)

> 'The Raja Guna should be known as the attraction quality that generates desires and which binds beings with attachment for duties.'**

***"Rajo Rāgātmakam Viddhi Trishnāsangasamudbhutam Tannivadhnāti Kaunteya Karmasangena Dehinam." (XIV, 7)

'Tama should be known to have evolved out of wrong ideas, Ajnana, which deludes all beings; it binds the beings through bewilderment, lethargy and sleep.'***

***"Tamastvajnānajam Viddhi Mohanam Sarva Dehinam Pramādalasya-nidrābhistannivadhnati Bhārata." (XIV, 8)

The Fifteenth Chapter is known as the *Purushottama Yoga* as in this chapter, for the first time, the idea of Purushottama has been introduced.

'In the world there are two types of Purusha, Indweller—the Perishable and the Imperishable; all the created beings are Perishable and Imperishable is the Kutastha. Uttama Purusha is different which is called the Paramatma—the Supreme Being. Who pervades all the three worlds, sustains and lords over and is Indestructible. As I am beyond the Perishable and better than the Imperishable hence I am described in this world and in the Vedas as the Purushottama.'ā

#"Dvāvimau Purushau Loke Ksharaschākshara Eva Cha Ksharah Sarvāni Bhutāni Kutasthohkshara Uchyate;" "Uttamah Purushastvanyah Paramātmetyudāritah Yo Lakatrayamāvishya Vibhartyavyaya lsvara;" "Yasmāt Ksharamatitohhamaksharādapi Chottamah Atohsmi Loke Vede Cha Pratithah Purushottamah." (XIV, 16, 17, 18)

The Sixteenth Chapter is named *Daivasura Sampad Vibhaga Yoga; in this chapter attitudes and aptitudes have been distinguished between divine, Daiva, and Satanic, Asura. Different propensities that draw man outwards have been described as Asura, while qualities and aptitudes that pull one inwards towards Self have been termed as divine or Daiva.*

The Seventeenth Chapter is called *Sraddha Traya Vibhāga Yoga. All human habits, his works, his food, his devotion have been distinguished into Satviki, Rajasik and Tamasik relating to the three Gunas.*

The last Chapter is styled as the Moksha Yoga, the Yoga of Emancipation. It is devoted essentially to the themes already developed in the earlier parts of the book. The following two verses from this chapter are not only devotional but also illustrative of the theme of the chapter.

'Oh, Arjun, the Lord exists in the heart of all beings; Who is moving all the beings by His Maya as if they are set on machines.'*

*"lsvarah Sarvabhutānām Hriddesherjuna Tishthati Bhrāmayan Sarvabhutāni Yantrārudhāni Māyayā." (XVIII, 61)

'Seek refuge in every manner in Him only; you can get the stage of unshakable existence and supreme bliss by His Grace!'**

**"Tameva Saranam Gaccha Sarvabhāvena Bhārata Tatprasādāt Param Santim Sthānam Prāpsyasi Sāsvatam." (XVIII, 62)

It can be seen that after describing various forces that constitute the opposing armies in the introductory First Chapter, the Gita offers superb lessons to warm up drooping spirit of the spiritual aspirant—first by emphasising impermanence of men and inevitability of death and destruction; the only lasting imperishable and indestructible Substance in the Universal picture being the Atma or the Self, the in-dwelling Spirit in all beings. Next the question of correct work that does not produce desire has been discussed in all its aspects. Desire is the cause of bondage of men and it is incorrect work which begets more and more work and desires. Subtleties of the created universe and of 'beings' are discussed in the next chapter detailing the relationship between the individual and the Universe, the microcosm and the macrocosm, underlying the basic conceptions of the Hindu Spiritual Culture. Sannyasa or renunciation, it has been explained, is not cessation of work but renunciation of fruits of work. A person may achieve perfect renunciation even by performing all work if he can withdraw himself and the senses, their functions done on their own under the attributes of Prakriti. The sixth chapter constitutes a brilliant discourse on the practice of Yoga stressing on the practical side of the question. Subsequent three chapters further deal with fundamental points of our culture.

Of the eighteen chapters of the holy book the second nine chapters, according to Sri Yukteshvar, contain wholesome expositions but as elaborations of the themes already dealt with and established in the first nine chapters.

Some hold that each of the eighteen chapters of the Gita relates to a particular feature of Kriya. Some others again opine that the eighteen chapters constitute three sextets, or three parts of six chapters each; the first six chapters constitute Karma Kanda, the second six chapters the Upasana Kanda and the last six chapters the Jnana Kanda.

When studied in their spiritual contexts, as given out in the Spiritual Interpretations by Sri Yukteshvar, correctness of the commentary by Nilakantha Suri, quoted earlier, is found to be aptly borne out.

3

Christ's Teachings And Hindu Scriptures

The most outstanding land mark and pioneering work of Swami Sri Yukteshvar in the realm of spiritual literatures has been his book "Kaivalya Darshanam—The Holy Science." Written at the instance of his Param Guru Babaji Maharaj, harmoniously blending the essences of the Hindu scriptures with the intrinsic teachings of Christ as contained scattered in different books of the Holy Bible, Holy Science is a novel treatise showing that the essential teachings of the two great religions—Hinduism and Christianity—are similar in contents. It may be relevant here to recall under what circumstances the idea of writing such a book was mooted.

In 1894 Swami Sri Yukteshvar, then Priya Nath Karar, went on a pilgrimage to Kumbha Mela then being held at Allahabad at the tri—junction the Ganga, the Jamuna and the sub-terranian Sarasvati; it was more for witnessing the big concourse of ascetics, saints and thousands of pious men and women that usually assemble at Kumbha, rather than for any desire to acquire religious or spiritual benedictions. But his bewildering experience and unbounded joy during this visit had been one of the greatest pilgrimages of his life, if not the greatest. He set up his residence at the Allahabad side of the river Jamuna. One day finding Allahabad side too crowded he crossed over to the opposite bank in a boat. This side was known as Jhusi. He was dressed like a Bengali gentleman in spotless Dhoti and a fashionable Punjabi with a walking stick in hand. He started strolling along the road which ran parallel to the river bank, musing over the similarities he had detected in the teachings of Christ with those of Hindu spiritual conceptions. Watching the huge assemblage of ascetics at the Kumbha he thought that there might be many in America and the West who although otherwise leading ordinary worldly life might possess spiritual potentialities which were no less than those of many of the ascetics present. While engrossed in such thoughts and walking on he suddenly heard a voice from behind uttering 'Swamiji Maharaj.' He found nobody near him and looked back from which direction the voice was coming. He saw a Sadhu, an ascetic, in saffron clothes waving his arm at him addressing him as Swamiji Maharaj and beckoning him towards him saying that Babaji was calling him. Priya Nath had not yet become a Sannyasi and as such could not expect anybody addressing him as Swamiji Maharaj. He thought some-body else had been meant. So deciding he continued to walk on as before. As he proceeded a few steps the same voice was heard again calling as before. He looked around but finding no other person near about he turned and walked up to the ascetic and charged, "I am not a Sannyasi, why are you then addressing me as Swamiji Maharaj?" The ascetic was taken-a-back but repeated that he had been called by Babaji and pointed to a tent situated not far away. Although surprised Priya Nath followed the ascetic into the tent. As he just entered the tent a very attractive looking saint of unusual radiance announced, "Swamiji Maharaj! take your seat." Priya Nath was perplexed at being addressed again as 'Swamiji Maharaj', this time by the strange saint mentioned as Babaji. Priya Nath bowed before the saint and taking his seat in front of him asked, "I am not a Sannyasi, why are you then calling me Swamiji Maharaj?" The mysterious saint burst into a laughter and replied, "Surely you are a Swamiji Maharaj; it has come out of my mouth! you are definitely a Swamiji Maharaj," and laughed out again. Priya Nath had no answer to such a surprising reaction.

Now that he was face to face with apparently a very highly spiritual saint Priya Nath took up the thread of what he was thinking all this time—his feelings that many worldly men of the west were possessors of at least same spiritual potentials as those of average ascetics congregated at the Kumbha. The saint who was listening smilingly nodded approval when Priya Nath had suggested this. Priya Nath then mentioned his new found secrets, that the Holy Bible contained certain observations which showed wonderful similarities with the basic conceptions of the Hindu scriptures. This time also the saint nodded his head in approval. A startling suggestion was then made by the mysterious saint; "You have been writing the Gita at your Guru's wishes; why not write a book at my behest on the lines you have now discussed," the strange saint remarked. Priya Nath was totally unprepared for such a development. He exclaimed in bewilderment, "What a suggestion Maharaj! I am totally unequipped and I lack intellectual acumen to accomplish such a serious task!" The saint who was smiling all this time now burst into laughter and said "It has come out of my mouth, and I know that this will be accomplished; no one ever refuse to do my behest," and laughed loudly again. Priya Nath did not know how to protest any more. At last he prayed, "If ever I succeed in writing such a book shall I have the favor of a Darshan from you Maharaj?" "Certainly" was the reassuring reply.

Priya Nath was very much impressed by his meeting the saint, although he did not know who this unusual saint was. He was, however, pleased to find at least one saint who agreed with his propositions of similarity between teachings of Lord Jesus and the basic teachings of the Hindu spiritual culture. Any way, he did not lay much importance and weight to what he had been told until he visited his Guru Lahiri Mahasay, soon afterwards, at Varanashi. After coming to Varanashi straight from Allahabad Priya Nath availed of the first opportunity to meet the Guru. Meeting him Priya Nath narrated his general experiences of his erstwhile visit to Kumbha Mela with great enthusiasm. Towards the end of the narration he repeated everything about his encounter with the strange and mysterious saint. After attentively listening to the account Lahiri Mahasay sat quiet and still as if in a trance for quite sometime, to the consternation of Priya Nath and a few others that were present at that time. Then the Yogiraj returned to his normal self again and looking at Priya Nath said, "You heard so many times about my Guru! Could you not recognise him? You were very lucky to have met my Guru Babaji." The entire episode now appeared in a completely unexpected and different shape to Priya Nath. He realised that what he had been asked to perform was not a casual opinion of an ordinary mendicant, but a holy commandment from the Guru of his own worshipful Guru! The entire perspective changed and he realised that he had been entrusted with a task which must necessarily be carried out. On his return home at Serampore Priya Nath's main occupation had been to formulate plans for writing the desired book and to collect required materials. The manuscripts were completed that very year and the book was named 'Kalvalya Darshanam, the Holy Science.'

The book was peculiarly designed; its texts were in Sanskrit in Devnagri script, as in other Hindu religious books, but they were elaborated in English with quotations at appropriate places from the Bible. It is a small book divided into four chapters. The first chapter has been designated as the Veda or the Gospel, the second as Abhishta or Goal, the third Sadhana or Procedure and the last Vibhuti or Revelations—all in a logical sequence.

Links or communication between Christ and the Wise men from the East has been a subject of speculations many times in history. Eighteen years of life of Jesus, known as the great Incognito, has been guessed by some as the period when he paid a return visit to the three wise Men from the East. Some

Yogis privately whisper that John the Baptist was a member of a secret society of Jerusalem who practised Kriya; and that Jesus had been taught Kriya by him. Nicholas Notovich was perhaps the first man in modern tines to bring to the notice of a surprised world that he found definite proof of Jesus' visit to Tibet and North Western part of India during his life time. His account contained in his book "The life of Saint Issa" (New York, 1890) is revealing. He claimed to have stumbled on to some very old manuscripts in the Himis Buddhist monastery in Ladakh, which contained records of the Messiah's visit to this part of the world, according to him, during the period between 12 and 30 years of his age.

Jawaharlal Nehru in his famous book 'Glimpses of World History' has mentioned at one place: "All over Central Asia, in Kashmir and Ladakh and Tibet and even further North, there is a strong belief that Jesus or Issa traveled about there.......there is nothing inherently improbable in his doing so."

In 1963 a controversy was publicly carried out in several issues of a renowned Bombay weekly over a very old tomb in Kashmir near Sri Nagar which was claimed by one opinion to be the tomb in which the mortal remains of Jesus had been interred; while another opinion vehemently opposed this. The newly published 'Suriya' magazine in its December, 1976 edition published an interesting article by Madhu Kapur giving some documentary evidence that the Rauzabal tomb at Sri Nagar was the holy sepulcher in which the mortal remains of Jesus the Christ were enshrined.

It goes to the searching analysis and deep insight of Swami Sri Yukteshvar, the credit of establishing close similarities between some of the Christ's teachings and the basic tenets of Yoga, thus showing that there was not only physical contact between Christ and India but there were cultural and spiritual exchanges as well. Hinduism and Christianity are the two great religions of the world, Christianity being the preponderant faith of the Western countries and vast population all over the world and Hindu scriptures, mainly written in Sanskrit, Sri Yukteshvar designed his book, in conformity with this fact, by writing the basic texts in Sanskrit and elaborating the essences of the texts in English, one of the major western languages.

Moreover, as will be evident from subsequent developments, the purpose inherent in the writing of the book was well served, by adopting this method.

It is said that Swami Sri Yukteshvar at one time had written a spiritual commentary on the Bible which, however, was not published. Once he spoke about it to a French gentleman who was holding some official position in the administration of the French settlement of Chandernagore with whom he had friendship. This Frenchman was very much impressed by what he heard and wanted to read the manuscripts himself. Accordingly the manuscripts were handed over to him. When the two met next time the Frenchman expressed that he had been overwhelmed by what he had read exclaiming, "You will revolutionise the entire Christiandom once these are published." He proposed that he might be permitted to take the manuscripts to Metropolitan France where he would like to show these to the scholars there, during his forthcoming visit on leave, promising to bring them back on return. Sri Yukteshvar agreed; but he did not get back the manuscripts as the Frenchman never came back to India again. The invaluable manuscripts were thus lost to futurity. Nobody knows what the commentaries were like as Sri Yukteshvar did not discuss the subject with anybody. However, he bequeathed to the grateful world in its place the Holy Science.

Veda-The Gospel

The First Chapter of the book, as the very title would indicate, contains what may be called axiomatic truths, propositions which are to be accepted without question. They form the basic premises on which the edifice of his thesis had been built. The very first text in this Chapter reads:

> "Sat, the One without a second without beginning and end is Param Brahma the only Substance that exists."*
>
> *"Anadyanantam Brahma Paramam Tadekamevadvitiyam Sat."

The above is an axiomatically accepted faith of both the Hindu and the Christian religions. The word Sat is derived from Sanskrit root meaning 'that which exists'.

Swami Sri Yukteshvar introduced the following quotation from the Bible to show the parallelism:

> "Now faith is the substance of things hoped for the evidence of things not seen." (Hebrew—XI, 1)

The second proposition offered in this chapter is that there are two aspects of 'Sat,' the Only Substance that exists, 'Chit' and 'Ananda'. They are the Positive and Negative components which are the Omniscient Love or Sarvajna Prema Veeja—the Holy Spirit—the attraction, and the Omni Potent Force or Sarva

Shakti Veeja Ananda the repulsion respectively. The former is comprehensible as love or attraction in man and the latter as will or enjoyment.

The Sarva Shakti Veeja Ananda in its aspect of repulsion vibrates, as a result of which emanates a stream of sound or Nada which is the 'celestial song' or Amen of the Christians and Pranava or the Shavda Brahma of the Hindu Shastras. Concomitant with the manifestation of this sound also manifest the ideas of Time, Space and of Units. These four ideas of Sound, Time, Space and Unit lay down the fundamentals on which the edifice of creation is built, which together act as a shroud or veil reflecting the Spiritual Rays of the Omniscient Love Prema Veeja, instead of comprehending them. This interplay of these two aspects of Divinity causes creation of chains of ideas culminating in the universal scene. While this shroud or cover has been termed as Maya or Delusion collectively and Avidya or Ignorance as its units in the Hindu Shastras, in the Biblical language the four ideas are described as 'four beasts in the midst and around the throne' of God the Father. The Spiritual Rays of the Holy Spirit reflected by Maya the cover, are particles of the Spirit Itself which constitute what is known in the Samkhya philosophy as Purusha and as Sons of God in the Bible. The Omniscient Love—the Holy Spirit however, continues to exercise attraction over Maya subjecting it to processes of deformations. The Biblical reference is as follows:

"And in the midst of the throne and round about the throne were four beasts full of eyes before and behind." (Revelation—IV, 4)

The above mentioned four beasts with 'eyes before and behind' have parallel conception in the Hindu concepts as well; the sphere of Maya, of the Pranava sound, is called the 'door' connecting the realms of Creation and the realms of the Spirit. This will be elaborated herein after.

Chit, the Omniscient Love, although reflected by the 'Cover' Maya instead of being comprehended brings about gradual changes in the 'cover' under its Divine attraction. The formations resulting in consequence thereof have been described in the book as those as laid down in the Samkhya Philosophy as Twenty Four Principles or Essences—the Chatur Binshati Tattva. The 'Cover', Maya, has been described as being composed of three Gunas or qualities of Sattva, Raja and Tama (Scient, Kinetic and Static) which remain in a state of equilibrium in Maya, the Delusion and also known as the Unmanifest, the Avyakta. Prakriti under the attraction of the Holy Spirit, the Omniscient Love Prema Veeja, the state of equilibrium of the three Gunas get disturbed and polarised resulting in a chain of deformations.

The first consequence of this deformation is the manifestation of the idea of Self or Atma and is described in the Samkhya as Mahat Tattva, the Mahat Brahma of the Gita in which the Divine 'casts' its seeds of creation of all beings—the 'womb' of the Creator.

Mahat Tattva next gets further deformed manifesting the Ego, Ahamkara, the Divine Ego (as apart from the ego in man) when the idea of separate existence dawns. This Ahamkara is the equivalent of the 'Son Of Man' in the Bible. The process of 'attraction' by the Omniscient Love, Chit, being a continuous feature deformation or Vikriti of the different stages of the chain of deformation of the Prakriti also continue. Thus with the manifestation of Ahamkara the three Gunas that constitute Prakriti (in a state of equilibrium) become distinctly 'precipitated' like the poles of magnetic materials such as iron filings when placed in a magnetic field. Sattva Guna constitutes the positive pole in this case which is the scient principle the 'revealer'; Tama Guna is the negative pole which is static principle and is the opposite of Sattva. Raja Guna the kinetic principle constitutes the neutral pole, or as Swami Sri Yukteshvar described, the neutralising pole. It is the Raja Guna under the impact of attraction of the divine Omniscient Love, Chit, becoming active that causes manifestation or precipitation of the other two Gunas. The above 'polarisation' of the Gunas forms the subtle base of the process of creation.

The three Gunas, although distinguished by their distinctive features, are but conglomerates of the same three Gunas in differing proportions.

Thus in Sattva Guna, which is the 'Scient' principle, Sattva preponderates over Raja and Tama; while in Raja Guna, the 'Kinetic' principle, the Raja preponderates over the other two. Similarly in the Tama Guna the 'Static' principle, Tama preponderates over Sattva and Raja. Intermediate stages in between the three 'precipitated' Gunas, the Sattva-Raja and the Raja-Tama, are also similar conglomerates of Sattva, Raja and Tama in differing proportions. The above five stages of Sattva, Raja, Tama, Sattva-Raja and Raja-Tama are the *Five Fundamental Essences, the Pancha Tattva, of the Samkhya philosophy which form the subtle*

base of creation. From the Sattva components of the above five states evolve the five subtle senses of Sight, Taste, Sound, Touch and Smell; the five Raja components give rise to five subtle organs of action and the five Tama components the five subtle objects. The five subtle organs of senses are the Pancha Jnanendriya, the five subtle organs of action are the Pancha Karmendriyas and the five Tama components, five subtle objects of sight, taste, sound, touch and smell—the Pancha Tanmatra. The Sattva Guna that gets polarised from Ahamkara is called Buddhi or Sattva Buddhi, the un-folder of the Divine content, the Intelligence, and the Tama its opposite that covers is called Anandatva or the Mind. The five Sattva components of above five stages aggregating together form the 'mind'; and the five Raja components of the polarised Ahamkara together constitute the Vital Flux, Prana.

The afore-mentioned Pancha Tattva is known as the *Causal Body, Karana Sharira* of Purusha, and the other Tattvas such as Ahamkara, Sattva Buddhi, Manas or mind, five subtle organs of senses, five subtle organs of action and the five subtle objects or Tanmatras constitute the *Fine Material Body, Sukshma Sharira.* The five Tanmatras or subtle objects after getting further deformed evolve five matters of earth, water, fire, air and vacuum—the *Five Great-Elements, the Pancha Mahabhutas.* These elements together constitute the *Gross Material Body or the Sthula Sharira of Purusha.*

It is, therefore, evident as proposed in the Holy Science, that the scheme of creation originates from the manifestation of the celestial sound Pranava under the Divine Love resulting in the different stages in the creation chain. Parallelism available in the Holy Bible in this respect is remarkable.

> *"These things, sayeth Amen, the faithful and true witness the beginning of creation of God." (Revelation—III, 15)*

> *"In the beginning was the word, the word was with God and the word was God." (John—I, 1)*

> *"All things were made by Him, and without Him was not anything made was made." (John—I, 3)*

> *"And the word was made flesh and blood among us." (John—I, 14)*

It is surprising to find that what has been explained by different Hindu Shastras have been so precisely and concisely depicted by the above Biblical sayings.

The aforementioned twenty four essences, the Chaturvinshati Tattvas, which are the different stages of unfoldment of the creation chain have been described in the Bible as 'twenty four seats' around the throne of God with twenty four elders sitting on them.

> "And round about the throne four and twenty seats and upon the seat I saw four and twenty elders." (Revelation—IV, 4)

The above expositions in the Holy Science will be found to be in conformity with the teachings of the Gita with some elaborations. As discussed in the chapter on the Spiritual Interpretations of the Gita the relevant verse is the one in the eighth Chapter.

> "Param Brahma is the Imperishable, the Nature Prakriti is the Self in where It dwells; the evolver of ideas of beings, Visarga (the Shabda Brahma or Pranava) is called Karma." (Gita—VIII, 3)

After expounding the basis of creation as above the Veda chapter of the extra-ordinary book suggests the next stage of the Divine Game. With the three bod-ies—Causal, Fine and Gross—having been formed the play of Repulsion comes to a halt and Attraction of the Divine Omniscient Love Prema Veeja becomes evident; the Gross matters formed as the end results of the creation chain are drawn together by Its pull creating the visible world of suns, stars and planets and of landscapes, seas, mountains and the rest and ultimately of insects, birds, reptiles and animals.

Pancha Kosha

The things created in the above manner are considered as the Purusha, the Son of God, having been encased in a series of five sheaths or whorls. By the Attraction of the Omniscient Love, Prema Veeja, these sheaths unfold one by one evolving different specimens of life. In the vocabulary of the Vedanta the Pancha Kosha, the five sheaths are called Annamay, Pranamay, Manomay, Vijnanamay and Anandamay Koshas.

Annamay: is the outermost shell, derived from the Sanskrit root Atti meaning to eat. It is the sphere of constant change—one thing getting destroyed but forming, another. It provides for nourishment or 'food' for the subsequent evolution. With the lifting of the shroud Annamay, living organisms like plants appear in the Pranamay which is the core of life.

Pranamay has been the very core of life; all vegetation are said to be expressions of Prana on life. This sheath also gets unveiled under the pulling effect of the Divine Love opening the veil over to the sphere of the mind, the Manomay.

Manomay is the realm of creatures and the animal world. The beings in this sphere are not only endowed with functions of life but also with functions of the mind allowing them to move about applying will and volition in addition to capacity for growth and reproduction.

Vijnanamay Kosha: When the Manomay Kosha is pierced under the Divine process of Attraction the next sheath is touched in which the 'beings' are also endowed with the gift of intelligence. This is the stage where man is evolved with all his attributes of intelligence and expertise in addition to attributes of life and mind.

Propelled by his intelligence he not only lords over the material world but pines for more and more satisfaction. In the end finding no satisfaction in material riches he searches for peace and lasting happiness. If one is fortunate enough he may meet a real teacher, a Sad Guru, who shows him the path to shatter the world of his Intelligence and lift him above this sphere.

Anandamay is the last sheath of the being which still keeps him shrouded from the Divine Spirit. A person who can reach this stage becomes engrossed in perpetual bliss and is likened unto an Angel. By remaining continuously in the ecstasies of joy and peace this last veil is also lifted and he is lifted above the veils of the Koshas and becomes identified with the reflections of the Spirit, the part and parcel of the Spirit Itself. He now becomes a completely free man, a true Sannyasi and a Christ, the Son-of-God.

Sapta Sargas

In Vedanta the entire picture thus far enumerated has been differentiated into seven separate spheres or Sargas or Lokas. They are Bhu, Bhuva, Sva, Maha, Jana, Tapa and Satya Lokas.

Bhu Loka is the visible world of beings characterised by sequences of appearance and disappearance under the inexorable laws of nature. It constitutes what has been described as the Gross Material Body, Sthula Sharira.

Bhuva Loka is the sphere of Fine Matters like the electrical attributes with absence of visible matters. Hence it is called the *Sunya* or the *Vacuum*. Subtle Indriyas, the organs of senses and of action, belong to this sphere.

Sva Lok is the realm of absence of all material ingredients of creation, gross or fine; hence it is called the Maha Sunya, the Great Vacuum. It is characterised by presence of what Swami Sri Yukteshvar termed Magnetic forces.

Bhuva and Sva Lokas together may be said to constitute the Sukshma Sharira or Fine Material Body.

Maha Loka is the sphere of the 'celestial song' or the Pranava, the Omkara. It lies between spheres of the Spirit and of creation and hence termed as the Link or the Door, the tenth door, Dashama Dvar of the Hindu conceptions. In terms of the Biblical versions this is the sphere of the four beasts in the midst and round about the throne of the Father with eyes before and behind.

Why it is called the Tenth Door in the Hindu concepts will be understood when seven other spheres known as Sapta Petals, the seven nether regions, are described. It is called the 'door' because from this sphere, and through the help of Pranava, one can rise above the realms of creation into the spheres of the Spirit. Hindu scriptures have spoken of the immense possibilities of remaining immersed in the Pranava sound.

We find the following affirmation in the Upanishadas in this respect.

> "Pranava is (likened unto) the bow, Self (I) is the arrow, Brahma is the target; the target may be hit by the unruffled and unwavering. One should remain in one-pointed attention on the arrow."*

> *"Pranavo Dhanu Sharohi Atma Brahma Tallakshyam Uchyate Apramattena Veddhavyam Sharavat Tanmayo Bhavet." (Kathopanishad)

Again:

> "Making Self the lower piece of Arani and Pranava the upper piece (the pair of wood for making fire) and practising rubbing (Pranava on Self) by Jnana the snares of bondage are burnt (by the fire thus generated)!"

Under the above concepts spiritual practices of the Hindus are directed towards manifestation of the Pranava and to remaining 'immersed' in that divine sound. In The Holy Science Swami Sri Yukteshvar has laid down in the chapter on Procedure, Sadhana, Pranava as the path for attaining and surrendering to Brahma—in conformity with the above.

Jana Lok is the sphere of Chaitanya or Purushas, the 'Reflected Spiritual Rays' described in the foregoing, the stage of the Sons of God. From here begins the realm of the Spirit beyond the realms of creation. The success of elevation to this sphere depends on the acquirement of capacity of remaining absorbed continuously in Pranava. The enlightened ascetics and sages endeavor to maintain this concentration for success in their spiritual efforts. He who succeeds becomes equivalent to a Son of God, a Christ. It is termed in Hindu scriptures as 'Alakshya' the Invisible.

Tapa Lok is the sphere of 'Eternal Patience', Tapa, of the Holy Spirit—the Altar of God, the Omniscient Love which 'attracts' the created beings to Its Altar and to the God the Father, the Only Real Substance that exists. It is called 'Agam', the Inaccessible, as man, as he is, cannot conceive of reaching this state.

Satya Lok is the Final and the ultimate state, which no one can think of or name; the Only Real Substance, the One without a Second—the Param

Purusha—that exists. As no one can define it, it is called 'Anam', the 'Nameless' in the Hindu scriptures.

Patals

The Hindu philosophies considered another set of spheres or stages which are called Sapta Patals which belong to the inner spheres of man. They do not refer to exterior nether worlds as commonly held. For terrestrial man there is no scope for fathomless deep, being creatures of a globe; by digging deeper and deeper, theoretically speaking, one would reach the surface on the other hemisphere. The Patals really mean the spots within men where Chaitanya or the Spirit can be specifically perceived. The Yogis call them Chakras or subtle circles of illumination. There are five such Chakras within the Sushumna, one in-between the eye-brows within and the last is called the Thousand-Petalled Lotus Sahasrar in the brain, the principal Seat of 'Chaitanya' in man. These are the seven Patals.

The Bible describes these Patals more eloquently in its own language.

> "...And being turned, I saw seven golden candlesticks."
> "And in the midst of the seven candlesticks one like the Son of Man."
> "And he had in his right hand seven stars..."
> "...The seven stars are the angels of the seven Churches; the seven candlesticks which thou sawest are the seven Churches."
>   (Revelation: I—1,12,13,16,20)

Man belongs to the Bhu Loka; and counting from the seven Chakras and going forward Bhuva Loka is the eighth, Sva Loka the ninth and Maha Loka becomes the tenth. Thus the name of this sphere as the tenth, Dasam, and being the sphere that provides the Link or door between the realms of creation and of the Spirit, it has been appropriately termed as the 'Tenth Door', Dasam Dvar.

The afore-mentioned fourteen spheres, seven Sargas and seven Patals, constitute what is called Chaturdash Bhuvana—the Fourteen Worlds—of the Hindu scriptures.

Man is inherently and inexorably drawn towards Divinity under the laws of the Divine, but he is unaware of it. He seeks solace and apparent happiness in things of the world. If perchance he meets a true guide, a preceptor who shows him the right path by 'opening his spiritual eye', which forms an essential part of initiation into Kriya Yoga, he may experience 'Inner Light'— Jyoti—and may be fortunate to get Pranava manifested. Pranava is the correct path which beckons the performer and lifts him up gradually above the different spheres and ultimately beyond the bounds and tentacles of creation. The correct teacher, the Sad Guru, is the essential first requirement to begin efforts in quest of spiritual enlightenment, and to an ardent seeker this becomes available under the Divine Law.

The Bible gives similar ideas but in a different way:

> "There was a man sent from God, whose name was John."
> "He was not that Light, but was sent to bear witness to that Light."
> "He said, I am the voice of one crying in the wilderness; Make straight the way of the Lord."
>
> (John: I—6, 8, 23)

Abishta, The Goal

The very first text in the second discourse of the book reads:

> "To get established in Self is emancipation."
> "Mukti Svarupe Avasthanam."

In the context of expositions in the preceding chapter, the above is a natural corollary. The Real Self is the Param Atma, the Only Real Substance that exists; all other features are but mere ideas worked on the Cover, Maya, culminating in man's appearance. His sufferings and pinings can only be dispelled when he can be free completely from the unreal ideas, which can be achieved by retracing the steps and getting back from where he has 'descended'. The aim or purpose of religion should also be same. The word religion has been derived from roots that mean 'to creep back', which is in conformity with the above proposition. In fact teachings of all major religions of the world, when properly scrutinised, are found to be directed to this end.

The word Dharma in the Hindu literatures convey similar conceptions, based on a different perspective. Dharma has been derived from Sanskrit root meaning 'that which holds'. It has been shown earlier that all apparent manifestations—the universal scene with all its attributes—have been possible and maintain their existence on the Ever-Existent, the All Pervasive and the Omni Potent Omniscient Param Purusha, the One without a Second. Awareness and identification with this Supreme Existence has been the goal of all spiritual efforts. The obstacles that an aspirant after this goal has to encounter have been described, in line with the propositions of the Patanjal Yoga Sutras, as Avidya, Asmita, Abhinivesha, Raga and Dvesha.

Avidya is the 'unit', or particle of the collective Maya, and is termed as Ignorance. This Ignorance is the first obstacle laid in the path of awareness and identification with Sat-Chit-Ananda, the Divinity, and the last to be overcome along the progress in the path to Self Realization.

Asmita has been defined, in conformity with Patanjal, as the unison of self the 'seer' (Drishi) and the 'seen' (Drik) that gives rise to evolution of the Ego, the Ahamkara inducting idea separateness in the Absolute. Like iron filings placed in an electro-magnetic field when magnetism is inducted in them Ahamkara gets 'polarised' into its Gunas or essential traits precipitating Intelligence and the Mind, Sattva Buddhi and Anandattva, and subsequent formations and attributes.

Abhinivesha is involvement and identification of self with the created feature as a consequence of the above.

Raga is attachment and attraction for certain objects and Dvesha is its opposite, revulsion for certain other objects, and,

Dvesha is its opposite, revulsion for certain other objects.

Overcoming of the obstacles depends on the realisation of Sat-Chit-Ananda, the Ultimate Reality. This can be realised, in the reverse order, through the process of Ananda, Chit and Sat.

Ananda can be realised from subtle spiritual experiences and spiritual ecstasies;

Chit can be comprehended from the 'effulgence' of Jnana by attaining Yoga or link with Self; and

Sat is realised as the All-Pervading and the Ever-Existent other than Which nothing else is comprehended, by completely surrendering to the 'Voice of God' the Pranava.

The different texts contained in this chapter closely conform to the relevant texts of the Yoga Sutras of Patanjali. Hence further elucidation on these may not be essential.

Sadhana, Procedure

With the elucidation of the goal of the spiritual aspirant in the context of the fundamental premise laid down in the chapter Veda the Gospel, curiosity naturally arises how this goal can be reached. In the third chapter, Sadhana, this aspect has been discussed.

The very first text in the chapter reads:

> "Tapah Svadhyaya Brahma Nidhanani Yajna." "Ascetic tolerance or patience, listening mentally digesting and forming correct ideas of Self constitute Svadhyaya consisting of Shravan, Manan and Nidhi Dhyasan and at last surrendering to Brahma is Yajna, holy work.

Those familiar with the Yoga Sutras will be struck by the similarity between what has been laid down in this treatise on Yoga and the above text in the Holy Science. There are two expressions, however, where the two texts differ. They are 'Ishvara Pranidhanani' and 'Kriya' in the Patanjal and 'Brahma Nidhanani' and 'Yajna' in The Holy Science.

Isvara has been defined in the Yoga Sutras as

> "The Special Purusha unaffected by Klesha (obstacles) Karma (efforts), Vipaka (wrong impressions) and Ashay (desires)."

> "Klesha Karma Vipaka Ashayair Aparamrishta Purusha Vishesha Isvara."

Yoga has been defined as "Stoppage of attributes of Chitta", and Kriya is naturally the technique or appropriate efforts directed towards achieving Yoga.

Isvara has been described in the discussion on the Spiritual Interpretation of the Gita as "chaitanya" in the Collective Causal Body (Karana Sharira under Maya) which does not conflict with the above definition in the Yoga Sutras.

The expressions in The Holy Science while having the same connotations, are more in line with the propositions in the Gita.

The expression 'surrendering to Brahma', in essence, does not basically differ. It may be recalled that Brahma has been stated as a 'being', a creation of the Almighty Divine, the one that evolves out of the Imperishable Param Brahma forming what has been described as the 'womb' in which the Lord casts Its seeds of creation.

Karma has been defined in the Gita as Pranava, the Shavda Brahmā, and is synonymous or co-existent with Yajna or holy work. It has been further stated that Brahma is always established in Yajna—"Nityam Yajne Pratishthitam."

In the above context exposition in The Holy Science would appear to be more direct and appropriate than what has been given in the Yoga Sutra referred to above.

Pranava has been expounded as the path for attaining Brahma Nidhan. The Yoga Sutras have defined Pranava as 'the expressor of Isvara'—"Isvara Vachaka", which fits in whatever has been said in the fore-going. Swami Sri Yukteshvar emphasised that the stream of continuous and unbroken sound of Pranava is essentially and spiritually the holy Ganga of the Hindus and the holy water of Jordan of the Christians. Getting absorbed in the stream of Pranava is equivalent to be 'born of water', according to the Bible, and lifting up beyond Pranava and effulgence of Jnana is equivalent to be 'born of the spirit'.

> "Verily, verily I say unto thee, Except a man be born of water and of the spirit, he cannot enter into the Kingdom of God." (John—III, 5)

How the Upanishadas have eulogised the efficacy of Pranava has been mentioned in the fore-going. There are many interpretations in the different scriptures including Chhandogya Upanishad where Pranava has been defined from a very wide perspective. But to the Kriya Yogis it is comprehensible as a continuous unbroken stream of sound of the gong, like an unbroken thin flow of oil when poured, which cannot be uttered by mouth.

> "Achhinnam Taila Dharamiva Deergha Ghanta Ninadavat Pranava Vyangam Yastam Veda Sa Vedavit." "Pranava sound is like the continuous sound of the gong unbroken like the flow of oil; and he who knows it is the Knower of Brahma."

To find out this divine path of Pranava one has to possess and acquire certain perquisites. These have been laid down, in line with the Yoga Sutras, as Shraddha, Veerya, Smriti and Samadhi.

Shraddha is the first perquisite which has been defined as:

> "Svabhavaja Premasya Vega Teevrata Shraddha." "Invigorating the intensity of the inherent love or attraction is Shraddha."

Every person is endowed with inherent divine gift of attraction for higher spiritual life. This ingrained trait has to be inculcated and enhanced for progress towards that goal. This can be done by keeping company of good men and following their examples and precepts. One should have the discretion to give up the company of a person whose instructions and precepts do not appear to give expected result. In this way by using scrutinising discretion one may be fortunate in finding a true teacher, a Sad Guru who will show him the correct path. The innate thirst for the Divine is bound to increase by devotedly following the precepts of the Sad Guru and by practising the techniques taught by him.

Veerya is prowess for patience and determination; it may be defined as 'nobility of heart.' To acquire Veerya one has to observe Yama and Niyama.

Yama consists of observances of abstinence from acts which tend to constrict one's heart and mental outlook—such as cruelty, dishonesty, greed, unnatural life and possessive propensity. These damaging traits have to be smashed by observing rigorous abstinence.

Niyama prescribes inculcating habits to keep the body and mind clean and enhance mental happiness, by feelingly and lovingly following the precepts of the Sad Guru and devotedly observing practises directed by him.

In this way by inculcating Niyama and observing Yama Veerya is established enabling the aspirant to acquire proper capacity to perform Asana, Pranayama and Pratyahara suitable for persons leading worldly life.

Asana is a sitting posture which imparts both steadiness and comfort.

In preparation for practising Pranayama one has to learn how to sit in proper posture so that the body remains straight and steady and at the same time subjected to no difficulty.

Pranayama is controlling of breaths, of the vital flux, the Prana. The practise is aimed at controlling the functions of the involuntary nerves particularly as those of the voluntary nerves can be controlled whenever one wishes. This control affords rest to the involuntary nerves which otherwise continue to be busy in their functions. This is very important for a healthy and long life.

Pratyahara: With the controlling of Prana senses gradually get withdrawn from their objects and turned inwards in the reverse direction towards the sensorium. This condition is known as Pratyahara.

Smriti: With success achieved in Pratyahara one attains more and more correct concentration which has been described as Smriti in The Holy Science. In the Yoga Sutras such a state is described as *Dharana*, and endeavors to maintain such state as *Dhyana*.

Samadhi has been defined as 'True Concentration'.

By his practice of Pranayama and Pratyahara the performer achieves better and better concentration; when the concentration is correctly made one is said to have attained Smriti; and true concentration is achieved when he becomes oblivious of everything else as well as his own identity when he is deemed to have attained Samadhi.

Samyama: The word ordinarily means control. With the advent of Dharana and Dhyana, of Smriti and of true concentration, Samadhi, the three stages arising in quick succession—one is considered to have achieved Samyama. This is also in conformity with the principles laid down in Yoga Sutras, which define Samyama as 'the three together jointly':

> "Trayorekatra Samyama."

The Holy Science has laid down that when Samyama is realised an enchanting stream of sound springs forth from within filling the heart of the performer with inexplicable joy. This is Pranava and this sound gradually becomes more and more refined and absorbing. The seeker after Self Realisation is instructed to continue to remain immersed in this heavenly sound. This condition is equivalent to 'dying' in one sense and to be 'born' into a new existence. Such a person is considered as 'twice born', a Dvija, in the Hindu concepts. To remain immersed in the holy sound constitutes 'Bhakti Yoga', the Yoga of correct devotion. It is through constantly and continuously remaining immersed in Pranava that one can gradually lift himself to higher and higher spheres of existence and ultimately beyond the veil of Maya, Delusion, into spiritual spheres. Such a consummation has been described in the Bible as being 'born of the Spirit'.

Progress of elevation described above is a step by step affair. The first step is elevation from Bhu Loka of gross matters to Bhuva Loka consisting of Fine Matters of which the subtle senses are composed; this occurs when one becomes a 'twice born' as explained above. The second step is the Sva Loka where even subtle senses and objects are absent; only effects of 'attraction' and 'repulsion' exist. This sphere has been termed by Swami Sri Yukteshvar as the Magnetic sphere as against the first step which has been termed as the Electrical sphere. The third step is the Maha Loka, the sphere of Pranava with the associated ideas of time, space and units. The step above this one is the first step into the realm of the Spirit, beyond the veil of Maya, Delusion. One must go through this step for further progress. The Bible contains the following affirmations in this context.

> "Jesus sayeth unto him, I am the way, the truth, and the life; no man cometh into the Father, but by me." (John—IV, 6)

".......Blessed are the dead that which die in the Lord henceforth." (Revelation—XIV, 13)

The above stage constitutes Jana Loka, the sphere of the Sons of Gods, of Spiritual Rays. From here one rises into the Tapa Loka, the sphere of the Holy Spirit, the Altar of God; and from thence to the ultimate stage, Satya Loka, when complete merger in the Infinite is achieved and completely emancipated in Kaivalya.

A great exponent of Yuga Dharma, of overall general effects of Yugas on men, Swami Sri Yukteshvar co-related the different features of human traits and behaviour, such as basic caste distinction, to the different stages acquired by a spiritual aspirant, a Kriya Yogi, in his spiritual path, and offered a more rational interpretation of the caste system. Thus any man born is a Kayastha and is in his personal Kali Yuga. Through observance of Yama and inculcation of Niyama he becomes a Kshatriya. When he meets a Sad Guru and is initiated into secrets of Pranayama and achieves manifestation of the Pranava he steps into his personal Dvapar Yuga and gets lifted into the 'Twice-Born', Dvija caste. By continuing to remain absorbed in Pranava one gets elevated up to Sva Loka and Maha Loka which is equivalent to getting into the Treta Yuga. Elevation above Maha Loka into Jana Loka and further up amounts to stepping into Satya Yuga when the individual is considered to have become a Brahmin.

It is evident that in this chapter Swami Sri Yukteshvar has not only prescribed a profound and potent procedure of spiritual efforts for realisation of the spiritual goal, but in the process has dexterously woven into the discussions his various thoughts and ideas on many social features and behaviour.

Vibhuti, Revelation

The concluding chapter of this remarkable book has been devoted to a discussion on the different experiences, subtle and unusual, that an aspirant after achieving spiritual enlightenment and emancipation from bondage does encounter; and hence the chapter has been appropriately named Revelation.

The first proposition made in this chapter is that proper steps should be taken to keep the body outfit healthy and clean, and to make the mind free from entanglements and rumblings. For this purpose recourses should be taken to proper use of Dravya (things), Oushadhi (medicine) and Mantra.

A Yajna aspirant should carefully choose his food so that only healthy and nourishing items are taken avoiding those that disturb and irritate the physical system. He prescribed that nutritious vegetarian diet was most suitable for man; human dentition indicates that man is born a vegetarian. Such food, he emphasised, was more suitable for men living in warm countries like India.

Whenever one suffers from any ailment he should consult health experts and take such medicines or such steps that they may suggest.

For making the mind free and clean Mantra should be adopted; Mantra is that which releases the mind, its acts of mentation (Mananat Trayate). Human breaths, the out-going and incoming, offer as the natural Mantra— the Yugala Mantra; this Mantra is the secret of practising Pranayama.

The first unusual experience a Yoga performer encounters is the manifestation of Pranava. As described in the chapter on Spiritual interpretation of the Gita Pranava is an unuttered and unutterable sound revealed to a Kriya Yogi when he is able to dive deeper in his concentration after practising Pranayama. To start with the sound comes out like the sound of the maddened black bees, refining gradually into a note like that of the flute, of the lute, of the gong and of thunder. With the manifestation of Pranava all senses and comprehensions get submerged making the Yogi achieve True Concentration or Samadhi.

With the revelation of Pranava the Kriya Yogi meets with subtle experiences such as light at the different Chakras or centers in the Shushumna along with their presiding 'deities', and at the Ajna Chakra in between the eye brows and at the thousand—petalled Sahasrar. These have been designated as the seven churches and seven angels that are perceived when one 'turns back', according to the Bible referred to in the foregoing.

Book with Seven Seals: When one is lifted into the Maha Loka, the sphere of Pranava, where under the 'Attraction' of the Holy Spirit—the Omniscient Divine Love—the Ego evolves and 'polarised', manifesting Intelligence (Buddhi), Mind (Manas) and the five fundamental essences (Panch Tattva) the seeker comes face to face with basic causes of creation where no other attributes are discernible. These five fundamental essences with the Mind and Intelligence constitute what has been likened unto a closed book. The Bible declares:

> "And I saw in the right hand of him that sat on the throne a book written within and on the back side, sealed with seven seals." (Revelation—V, 1)

Ascetic Majesties: What are commonly stated to be Ashta Siddhis displayed by saintly Yogis, have been described by Swami Sri Yukteshvar as Ascetic Majesties that an illumined Yogi automatically comes to possess by virtue of his elevation. This proposition gives a more rational clarification in the spiritual sense of the so-called miracles (not tricks) found displayed by exceptional ascetics.

It has been laid down in this chapter that when the seeker after divine life gets elevated above the limits of creation into Spiritual realms he comes face to face with Brahma, the Universal Creative Force, and gets linked with the Spirit. In such a condition he becomes Brahma-Like (Brahmaiva Bhavati) and as such becomes capable of all works applicable to Brahma. The holy Bible records this development more appropriately in the following:

> "Verily, verily, I say unto you, he that believeth on Me, that work I do shall he do also; and greater works than these shall he do; because I go unto my Father." (John—XIV, 14)

> "As many as received Him, to them gave He power to become Sons of God, even to them that believe on His name." (John—1, 12)

The Ascetic Majesties have been shown as of eight kinds; Anima, Mahima, Laghima, Garima, Prapti, Vaseetva, Prakamya and Isitva.

Anima is the power to make one's body or anything as minute as a particle or atom;

Mahima is the power to make the body or any object as large as he wishes;

Laghima is the capacity to make the body or anything as light as he likes;

Garima is the majesty of making the body or any objects as heavy as he wishes;

Prapti is the power to obtain whatever he desires;

Vaseetva is the power to bring anything and everything under subjugation and control;

Prakamya is the ability to satiate all desires; and

Isitva is power to lord it over anything and everything.

The above powers, the Ascetic Majesties, are real capacities that very highly advanced Yogis may acquire automatically and are not trickeries. But they are not meant for exhibitionist purposes. When a saint of this high stature becomes moved by any sight or petition his poise in the Infinite gets momentarily disturbed, and according to Divine law all powers in the Universal scheme rush at such a moment to fulfill the desire of the saint to re-establish him in his endless calm and poise.

A saint of this stature is one who is always 'linked'; he is an emancipated soul—a Jivan Mukta. He can maintain his mortal form as long as he wishes; he dies only whenever he wishes that it is time for casting off the long-used body and close the chapter. Deciding thus he surrenders to the Holy Spirit, the Altar of God, and merges into the Infinite, the Ever-Existent Param Atma and attains Kaivalya, complete emancipation.

The Bible contains a similar affirmation as shown below:

> "To him that overcometh will I grant to sit with me in my throne even as I also over came and am set down with my Father in His throne." (Revelation—III, 21)

After carefully considering the different discussions contained in the Kaivalya Darshanam, The Holy Science one is convinced that the mysterious assignment received by Swami Sri Yukteshvar from his Param Guru Babaji Maharaj in the mysteriously 'arranged' meeting at Allahabad during Kumbha Mela celebrations of 1894 has been admirably accomplished with consummate skill, masterly logic, erudition and deep insight. It is remarkable that Paramhansa Yogananda who had carried the message of Kriya Yoga to America based his teachings in that country on the teachings contained in the Holy Science.

4

The Yuga

Yuga is a Hindu conception closely and severally linked with various cultural thoughts and religious beliefs and practices. Yugas consist of immense lengths of time, counted in thousands of years. Standards of measuring and expressing the lengths of time also gives an insight into the Hindu conception.

It does not need mentioning that the current measure of time—of hour, minute and second has—been determined by dividing the duration of time between two consequitive sunrise by twenty four, which is the hour; dividing the hour by sixty determining the minute and then dividing the minute by sixty again to get the second. The period of twenty four hours between two consequitive sunrise, needless to state, constitute a day and a night, an Aho Ratra. The Shastras lay down several kinds of Aho Ratra conditioned by sequences of appearance and disappearance of certain specific feature. Thus a sequence of appearance and disappearance of sunlight is the measure of a human Aho-Ratra. Similarly we have Aho Ratra of the Pitris (Manes), Aho Ratra of the Devas and Aho Ratra of Brahma.

Twinkle of the eye is taken as the unit measure of time and Aho Ratra of man is arrived at by a series of multiplication. According to Manu Smriti the equation is as follows;

> "Ten and eight twinkles make one Kashtha, thirty Kashthas make a Kala; Thirty Kalas make a Muhurta and similar (count) make an Aho Ratra."*

> *"Nimesha Dasashtaucha Kashtha Tringshat Tu Ta Kala Tringshat Kala Muhurta Shyat Aho Ratra Tu Tavata."

Other types of Aho Ratra, according to Manu Smriti, are also dependent on the sun:

> "The sun delineates Aho and Ratra—Day and Night for men and the gods; night is for sleep of beings and day for efforts for work"**

**"Aho Ratra Vibhajate Suryo Manusha Daivike Ratrah Svapnaya Bhutanam Cheshtayai Karmanamahah."

Processes of sequence of 'activity' and 'rest' of specific features are the criteria by which the other Aho Ratras are recognised.

Aho Ratra of the Pitris: Pitris are commonly held to be supernatural beings who exist in between men and gods after death, the Manes. Swami Sri Yukteshvar held that the 'abode of the Manes' was a fiction, and that the word Pitri in reality meant that which was inherited from the Pitris, the parents; Pitri Lok, according to the Swami, was the human body inherited from parents.

"Pitrye Ratryahani Masa Vibhagastu Pakshayo Karmacheshtasvaha Krishna Sukla Svapnaya Sarvari." "Day and Night (Aho Ratra) of the Pitris is the month divided into Pakshas (two fortnights); The dark fortnight (Krishna Paksha) is the Day for activity and the bright fortnight (Sukla Paksha) is the Night for sleep."

Swami Sri Yukteshvar held that during a period of a month, a lunar month, flesh and blood in the human body (inheritance from the parents) get replenished and refreshed through the process of 'activity' and 'rest'; and that the above Aho Ratra of Pitris relates to that phenomenon. In the sphere of insects also there is a class, the honey bees, who are noticed to keep busy during the dark fortnight of the month collecting honey from flowers and to take rest inside the honey combs during the bright fortnight; for them, therefore, the former fortnight is the Day and the latter the Night.

Aho Ratra of the Devas: The general belief is that the Devas are the dwellers in the heaven. Swami Sri Yukteshvar explained that this was a wrong notion. Actually the Devas represent the subtle senses, the Fine Matters, which are not subject to laws of gross matters. The Upanishadas at many places used the word Deva to indicate Indriyas, the subtle senses. Aho Ratra for the Devas has been defined in the Manu Smriti as follows:

"The year again is delineated as Day and Night of the Devas; there Uttarayan is the Day and Dakshinayan is Night."*

*"Daive Ratri Ahani Varsham Pravibhagastayo Punah Ahastatra Udgayanam Ratrjshyat Dakshinayanam."

The period of six months of the year from the twenty fifth of December when the sun appears to move Northward from its Southernmost limit toward North is called Uttarayan and the remaining six months when the Sun apparently moves Southwards from its Northernmost position is called

Dakshinayan. As during the former half year the Sun comes towards the North, toward Aryavarta, the land of the Hindus, Hindu savants considered it to be an auspicious period. It is assumed that finer elements like the subtle senses remain fresh and active during this period and as such more propitious for religious rituals and spiritual experiences. It may be recalled that in the story of the Maha Bharata the Kaurava hero Bhishma when lying on a bed of arrows preferred to wait till the advent of Uttarayan to breathe his last. This period of six months hence is considered as the Day of the 'Devas'. The remaining half of the year when the Sun gets going towards the South and away from the home of the Hindus has been said to constitute 'their' Night.

Aho Ratra of Brahma and the Yugas:
Shrimad Bhagavad Gita defined Aho Ratra of Brahma as under:

> "Those who know Brahma's day as of one thousand Yugas and night also as duration of one thousand Yugas are the 'knowers' of Aho Ratra."*

> *"Sahasra Yugaparyantamaharyad Brahmano Viduh Ratri Yuga Sahasrantam Te Aho Ratra Vido Janah." (Gita—VII, 17)

Manu Smriti, which has dealt with this subject in much greater details however, has introduced the idea of different Yugas before defining Aho Ratra of Brahma. It says:

> "Comprehend now proofs of Day and Night of Brahma including one by one, in short, of the Yugas."**

> **"Brahmasya Tu Kshapahasya Yat Pramanam Samasata Ekaikaso Yuganamtu Kramasah Tannivodata."

Manu Smriti then defines the different Yugas:

Ordinary Yugas—Satya, Treta, Dvapar and Kali:

> "Four thousand years constitute a Krita (Satya) Yuga, it has its Sandhya and Sandhyangsha (mutation periods of Yuga dawn and Yuga dusk) of same duration; the remaining three (Yugas) and their Sandhya and Sandhyangsha are progressively shorter by one in thousands and hundreds."***

> ***"Chatvaryahu Sahasrani Varshanam Tu Kritam Yugam Tasya Tavat Sati Sandhya Sandhyangshashcha Tathavidhah Itareshu Sasandheyshu Sasandhyangsheshu Cha Trishu Ekapayena Vartante Sahasrani Satani Cha."

After giving out the length of the Satya Yuga, Manu states that the other three Yugas—the Treta, Dvapar and Kali—should be less by one in number at every step. The periods of mutation, the Yuga dawns and the Yuga dusks, are in hundreds of years but of the same numbers, and are also to be progressively less by one in the subsequent Yugas.

According to above, duration of the four Yugas will be as follows:

Yuga Name	Yuga Age	Period of Sandhya	Period of Sandhyangsha	Total Period
SATYA YUGA	4,000 yrs.	400 yrs.	400 yrs.	4,800 yrs.
TRETA YUGA	3,000 yrs.	300 yrs.	300 yrs.	3,600 yrs.
DVAPAR YUGA	2,000 yrs.	200 yrs.	200 yrs.	2,400 yrs.
KALI YUGA	1,000 yrs.	100 yrs.	100 yrs.	1,200 yrs.
Total for the four yugas				12,000 years

Daiva Yuga:

The aggregate of the length of the four Yuga periods is twelve thousand years, as can be seen. Manu Smriti defines this period as Daiva Yuga.

> "This which has been enumerated about the four Yugas, this twelve thousand years constitute a Yuga of the Devas."*

> *"Yadetat Parisankhyatam Adaveva Chatur Yugam Etaddvadasa Sahasram Devanam Yugam Uchyate."

Thus a Daiva Yuga has been defined as the aggregate of the periods of the four Yugas, of twelve thousand years.

Aho Ratra of Brahma:

Description of Aho Ratra of Brahma as found in the Gita, already quoted, is same in content as that in the Manu Smriti except that the latter has mentioned Daiva Yuga in place of simply Yugas in the Gita. Moreover Manu Smriti gives its relation with the ordinary Yugas.

> "One thousand Daiva Yugas in number should be known as the Day of Brahma and a similar period as the Night."*

> *"Daivikanam Yuganamtu Sahasram Parisankhyaya Brahmamekam Ahar-jneyam Tavati Ratrirevacha."

Day of Brahma would indicate that the Universal Creative Force, Brahma, remains active or awake during the period of one thousand Daiva Yugas of twelve thousand years each. This period is known as a Kalpa. Another period of one thousand Daiva Yugas is the period of Night of Brahma indicating that during this period the Universal Creative Force goes into 'rest' or 'sleep' when creation is withdrawn. The Day of Brahma again dawns after the lapse of this condition of Brahma's Night. The Gita in the seventh chapter has described this feature very specifically. To quote:

> "All 'beings' are manifested out of the Unmanifest (Prakriti) at the advent of the Day; at the advent of Night (the same) dissolve into the same, called the Unmanifest;" "All these beings are born again and again and are dissolved at the advent of the Night and are born again at the end of Night without any compulsion."**

> **"Avyaktadvyaktaya Sarvah Prabhavanti Aharagame Ratryagame Praliyante Tatraiva Avyakta Samjnake." "Bhutagramah Sa Evayam Bhutva Bhutva Praliyate Ratryagame Avashah Partha Prabhavantyaharagame." (Gita—VII, 18 & 19)

Manu Smriti has given out further yardsticks of measuring the limitless time confirming at the same time the above exposition of the Gita. Manu Smriti continues:

> "What has been stated earlier as Daiva Yuga of twelve thousand years, Seventy one times of that is called a Manvantara; "Manvantaras are innumerable for both creation and dissolution, The Great Benefactor (Divinity) makes them again and again like a game of toys."***

> ***"Yat Prak Dvadasa Sahasramuditam Daivikam Yugam Tadekasaptatigunam Manvantaramihochyate" "Manvantaranyasankhyani Sarga Samhara Evacha Kridadannaivaitat Kurute Parameshthi Punah Punah."

It is evident from the above extensively quoted texts from the Manu Smriti that the Hindu conceptions of measuring time and expressing it in terms of Day and Night is a unique feature. The traditional literatures and almanacs contain frequent references to these concepts. From the last two quotations it is stipulated that in a Kalpa of one thousand Daiva Yugas there should at least be fourteen periods of Manvantara; each such period is said to be presided by a Manu. The almanacs give names of fourteen Manus, the name of the present Manu being Vaivasvata Manu and that the present era is about in the middle of the present Kalpa.

Traditional ideas in this respect however, do not conform to the interpretation of Swami Sri Yukteshvar which is based on the texts of the highly respected religious literature, the Manu Smriti. According to the traditionalists the age of a Yuga should be counted by considering the Varsha as the Daiva year. This would make the age of Kali, as an example, consist of twelve hundred

Daiva years—each Daiva year being made up of three hundred and sixty Daiva days and nights, each Daiva day being a normal year of 360 days. Thus the total period of the age of the Kali Yuga is to be (1200 x 360) 432,000 years. Similarly age of the other Yugas has to be multiplied by three hundred and sixty giving astronomical figures as the age of these Yugas. Swami Sri Yukteshvar vehemently opposed this stand and showed that this view was not only contrary to the scriptures but also against astrological calculations and logical thinkings.

It is abundantly clear from the above quotations from the Manu Smriti that two types of Yugas have been recorded, the ordinary Yugas of Satya, Treta, Dvapar and Kali and Daiva Yuga; both the varieties having been expressed in terms of years only and not in terms of any Daiva years. There is no scope, therefore, for any confusion in this regard. The stand of the traditionalists would appear, as such, to be wrong and groundless.

Characteristic of the phenomenal universal scene is its incessant movement. Everything created is constantly on the 'move' in one way or the other. The Sanskrit synonym of the word for universe, Jagat, meaning that which 'goes' or moves, gives a correct description of the reality. The earth rotates round its axis once every day causing Day and Night; it revolves round the Sun along its orbit once every year causing variation of seasons; and the moon revolves round the earth every month causing a month of two fortnights—the dark fortnight and the bright fortnight. Hindu Astrology conceived of another heavenly cyclic movement, this time of the Solar system; the Sun with its planets and satellites, in relation to what is said to be the Grand Centre of the Universal Creative Force, the Vishnu Nabhi or the navel of the Lord Protector of creation Vishnu. This movement causes appearance and disappearance of Yugas.

Rotational diurnal movement of the earth round its axis brings one half of the globe alternately facing the Sun and the other half to the opposite side. For the side that faces the sun it is then day and for the opposite side it is night. In its yearly revolution round the Sun the axis of the earth remains at an inclined position making an angle of about sixty six and half degree with the orbit and moves in such a manner that the changing positions of the axis are always parallel. This makes the Northern and the Southern hemispheres of the earth alternately coming closer and moving further away from the Sun causing changes of seasons.

The moon has no rotational movement; it revolves round the earth keeping one side constantly facing the sun. This creates, conditions for the moon to appear in different phases. In the course of its movement the moon oscillates as it were between a nearest point and the farthest from the Sun; when it comes to the nearest point its position is in-between the Sun and the Earth and hence its dark side faces the earth. This is the New Moon, Amavasya. When the moon reaches the farthest point and is placed on the other side of the earth its bright side becomes fully visible. This is the Full Moon. In the cyclic movement of the Solar system the Sun with its family of planets and satellites moves toward the Universal Grand Centre from the farthest point, and as it comes nearer and nearer to the Centre of the Universal Creative Force the inherent virtues, Dharma, get manifested in men signifying advent of higher and higher Yugas. When the system is at the farthest distance from Vishnu Nabhi the earth is said to be in the Kali Yuga. Proceeding towards the Grand Centre, thus coming closer and closer to its spiritual aura, the earth passes through Dvapar and Treta and to the Satya Yuga. Continuing the cyclic movement as the Solar system goes away farther and farther from the Grand Centre it gets into less and less potent Yugas of Treta, Dvapar and the Kali.

According to Hindu conceptions virtues, Dharma, are fourfold—Chatushpad; in the Satya Yuga all the four-fold virtues remain fully manifested, but in the subsequent Yugas they decrease by one fold in each culminating in only one kind of virtue in the Kali Yuga. Swami Sri Yukteshvar interpreted these virtues as Spiritual, Magnetic, Electrical and Material. As such all the four kinds are manifest in Satya Yuga; in Treta the Spiritual virtue gets submerged leaving the other three kinds manifested; in Dvapar Electrical and Material virtues remain manifested while in the Kali only the Material virtue remains. Hence Kali is known as the Dark Age.

While Hindu scriptures in this respect refer to the sequence of the Yugas in the descending order—from Satya to Treta, Dvapar and Kali—no reference is found on the changes suggested above in the ascending order from Kali to Dvapar, Treta and Satya. The common belief is that after the end of Kali Yuga the world would face a catastrophe after which Satya Yuga will dawn. Such quadruple jump from Kali to Satya is against what is observed in all natural laws of changes, and as such inconceivable.

It may be reiterated that in a complete cycle of movement of the sun with its planets and satellites there are two sets of Yugas of Satya, Treta, Dvapar and Kali thereby forming two periods of Daiva Yuga of twelve thousand years each. In the process pairs of such Yugas have been formed—two Satya Yuga, two Treta, two Dvapar, two Kali and two Daiva Yugas. Yuga stands for 'pair', and as such naming the above as Yugas would appear appropriate and in keeping with actualities. The Surya Siddhanta, the oldest of the known Hindu Astrological documents, has termed the period of twenty four thousand years which is equivalent to the time taken by the Solar system to make a complete cycle as the Maha Yuga. The traditionalists, however, would not accept any suggestion that a Satya Yuga can follow a Treta a Dvapar and a Kali Yuga, as no reference could be produced from the old scriptures to that effect. The famous Sanskrit scholar and saint of Dhanbad, Late Ram Nath Shastri, who was personally known to Swami Sri Yukteshvar and one of his admirers, told this author that the Swami's thesis with regard to Yugas was superb; but as no reference could be traced in the ancient literatures about the ascending Yugas the strong traditionalists could not be persuaded to accept the thesis; and without the traditionalists agreeing the proposal could not be acceptable to the people at large.

Swami Sri Yukteshvar was very firm in his views on the matter and was convinced that the ideas of the traditionalists were faulty and based on wrong readings of the scriptural texts. He maintained that the wrong conceptions had crept in by wrong interpretations introduced by an early commentator of Mahabharata named Kulluk Bhatta, who was a creature of the Dark Age. Swami Sri Yukteshvar drew notice to another factor followed by the traditionalists to press the correctness of his thesis. They hold that at present the world is passing through five thousand and seventy eight years of the mutation period of Kali of its total period of thirty six thousand years (100 x 360); and that Kali proper is still more than thirty thousand years away (36,000-5078). However, there is no elucidation as to how this figure of 5078 had been arrived at. Swami Sri Yukteshvar contended that the figure was correct as far as the number of years was concerned but not the reference to which this was put to. He suggested that in very ancient times years were related to the Yugas they belonged to, in the same way as names of days of the week were related to planets and names of the Hindu months of the year related to important stars of the twelve constellations. He argued that years of Satya Yuga were counted from Satya 1 onwards up to Satya 4,800; the chronology then changed to Treta 1 up to Treta 3,600 and so on. When Dvapara 2,400 was completed and Kali years should have started the then people in authority in the capital of India elected to continue with Dvapar chronology. This was due to, he argued, king Yudhishthira's decision to leave his throne and worldly life at the advent of Kali Yuga which would not be a period fit to live in. When he left the capital his brothers, courteers and scholars of his capital followed him on his journey to the Himalayas. As a result, in the absence of scholars, the advent of Kali went un-noticed and hence the running chronology was persevered with.

As stated earlier the period of a Dvapar Yuga is 2,400 years. At the conclusion of this Yuga the previous chronology having continued during Kali the last year of Kali, according to the chronology would be 3,600. With the completion of the Kali Yuga in the descending order the ascending order of change in the Yugas start, and after passing through another twelve hundred years Dvapara would begin. The number 5,078 would show that not only was the Kali in the ascending order was completed but two hundred and seventy seven years of the Dvapar have also been over (5,078-1,200-3,600). Swami Sri Yukteshvar was of the view that world was now in Dvapara Yuga and that having completed its mutation period of two hundred years have passed into the Yuga proper, and that in the year 1978 A. D. is on its seventy eighth year.

Another Astronomical phenomenon known as Precession of the Equinox, Swami Sri Yukteshvar affirmed, had close relationship with the Yugas. Equinox occurs when the sun is exactly on the equator making duration of the day and night equal on that day. The point in the heaven or zodiac in the constellation at which equinox takes place is known as the equinoxial point. It has been observed by Astronomers from of old that the equinox does not occur at a fixed point every year; but that the equinoxial point precedes by a fraction of a degree every year. According to Surya Siddhanta the quantum of Precession was fifty four seconds (54") a year. Present day Astronomers, however, found this quantum to be a little less. Taking 54" seconds as the quantum it will take twenty four thousand years (360X60X60 divided by 54) for the equinox to occur again at the same point of the constellation. As seen above this period is equivalent to a Maha Yuga (Surya Siddhanta) and to two Daiva Yugas.

From his studies of Astrology and Vedic literatures Swami Sri Yukteshvar found that the last Satya Yuga ensued when the Autumnal Equinox occurred at the first point of the constellation Aries in the year 11,501 B.C. Thus a period of 13,477 years must have elapsed before reaching the year 1978 A.D, which is equivalent to a Daiva Yuga plus a period of Kali Yuga and another two hundred and seventy seven years. Calculating on the above basis Autumnal Equinox will take place again in the first point of Aries in the year 12,501 A.D. Equinoxial point is an observable factor and by observing the present position correctness or otherwise of the Swami's views can be verified. Swami Sri Yukteshvar opined that the Autumnal Equinox occurred at the present time some where in the constellation Libra.

There was another subject where Swami Sri Yukteshvar found fault with the traditionalists. This was in respect of certain festival days of the Hindu considered very auspicious. They are the four Sankrantis—, the two Equinoxes and the two Solstices. When the Sun in its path from its Southern limit to the North crosses the Equator, which takes place during Spring on the 23rd of March, Vernal Equinox occurs. The day the Sun comes exactly over the Equator duration of night and day becomes equal; hence the name. The Hindus call this Maha Vishuva Sankranti. Similarly when the Sun in its Southerly course from the Northernmost region crosses the Equator another equinox takes place; and as this occurs in autumn, in September, it is known as the Autumnal Equinox, Jala Vishuva Sankranti. The Sun moves, rather appears to move, between tropics of Capricorn and Cancer—which are, like the Equator, but imaginary lines. The above two tropics are the limits up to which the Sun can go either way. When the Sun touches the Southernmost limit which is the Tropic of Capricorn, the Makar Kranti, the Hindu festival Makar Sankranti is observed. On this day we have the longest night and the shortest day of the year, and hence can easily be distinguished. The Sun then takes up its Northerly course end, after crossing the Equator reaches its Northernmost limit, which is the Tropic of Cancer—Karkat Kranti; this day is observed as the Karkat Sankranti. We have on this day the shortest night and the longest day of the year, and as such is easily recognisable. The Sun moves again Southwards and crossing the Equator moves to the Southernmost tip of the journey. These are the four important Sankrantis of the year whose occurrence cannot be confused. But the Hindu almanacs stick to the old dates ascertained hundreds of years ago without caring to make any adjustment in accordance with the phenomenon of Precession of Equinoxes. As a result these festivals are wrongly observed when actual Sankrantis have already passed about three weeks ago.

Swami Sri Yukteshvar was not only a strong exponent of the new ideas of Yugas, as detailed in the fore-going, but also of the urgent necessity of reforming the Hindu almanac. The glaring example is observation of the Hindu New Year. According to tradition from the Vedic times new year begins on the day immediately following the Vernal Equinox, Maha Vishuva Sankranti. Although apparently the same tradition is still being followed, actually the present day new year begins about three weeks after the Vernal Equinox really occurs due to the above mistake. Swami Sri Yukteshvar had launched a country wide campaign meeting scholars and savants in important places like Varanashi and Puri and holding conferences where he placed his views and sought approval of the guardians of traditions to introduce the changes, both with regard to the Yugas as well as to reformation of almanacs in line with his findings. The hard conservative core, however, did not agree although they appreciated the Swami's arguments and logic of facts.

It does great credit to Swami Sri Yukteshvar's acumen and penetrating analysis, however, when after about half a century the independent Government of India set up a Commission for reforming the almanacs under the Chairmanship of the world famous scientist Dr. Meghnath Saha, who recommended that the New Year should begin on the eighth day of the month of Chaitra instead of the day following the thirty first day of Chaitra. But for a conservative people like the Indians who are strongly bound by traditional customs and usages any change is unacceptable even if recommended by the wisest of men. Recommendations of the Shah Commission has been under dusts in the national archives and New Year is continuing to be held as before on the first day of Vaisakh, about three weeks after the actual vernal equinox occurs.

To revert to suggestions put forward by Swami Sri Yukteshvar in regard to reckoning of Years. He suggested that the years should be reckoned in relation to their Yuga, and opined that this was the practice in ancient times. Like names of days of the week and of months of the year which are not associated with any personality or human events names of years should also be linked with natural and celestial phenomenon. Name of days of the week have been derived from the planets (Sun and Moon are reckoned as planets in Astrology). Ravivar (Sunday) from Sun (Ravi), Somvar (Monday) from Moon (Som), Mangal Var (Tuesday) from Mangal (Mars), Budhvar (Wednesday) from Budh (Mercury), Vrihashpativar (Thursday) from Vrihashpati (Jupiter), Shukravar (Friday) from Shukra (Venus) and Shanivar (Saturday) from Shani (Saturn). Similarly names of months have been derived from prominent stars of the different constellations. Thus Vaishakh has been derived from the star Vishakha, Jaishtha from Jyeshtha, Ashad from the Star Purvashada, Shravan from Shravani, Kartik from Kirtika, Agrahayan which is alternately known as Marga Sirsha from Mriga shira, Paush from Pusha, Magh from Magha, Falgun from Falguni and Chaitra from the star Chitra. In the same way years should also be linked with Yugas like Satya year, Treta Year and so on, Swami Sri Yukteshvar contended. He himself followed this principle in his own publications. The Holy Science written in 1894 was shown as having been written in 194 Dwapara. In all publications of different centres established under Swami Sri Yukteshvar's guidance the Yuga year was used side by side with Christian era.

The different cyclic movements of heavenly bodies that have been shown earlier to cause day and night, different seasons, dark and bright fortnights and Yugas are simultaneous. While the sun with its planets and satellites moves in relation to the Vishnu Nabhi the earth continues with its diurnal and annual movements and the moon keeps on revolving round the earth. One complete rotation of the earth round its axis constitutes the day, one complete revolution of the moon round the earth constitutes a lunar month, one complete revolution of the earth along its orbit round the sun constitutes the solar year and one complete cycle by the solar system in relation to the Universal Grand Centre constitutes the Daiva Yuga 'couple'. It is not difficult, therefore, to draw a co-relation between these different movements.

It has been found that a lunar month is slightly shorter than a solar month, and that a year has a few more days than twelve lunar months. In fact it has been found that three years are equal to thirty seven months. As the months are fixed on lunar basis some of the months are extended by a few more days every three years to conform to the years. Such months are known to almanac makers as Mala Masa, months with excess days. Taking thirty seven lunar months as equivalent to three years it is possible to describe Yugas in terms of lunar months. This standard assumes great importance in practical application in the spiritual technique of Kriya Yoga. It is from this aspect that a discussion on the Yugas is found to be relevant in a discourse devoted to Kriya Yoga.

It has been mentioned already that the Yugas indicate acquirement of different virtues, 'Dharma', and for such Dharmas to find expression requires elapse of thousands and thousands of years of time. The ancient Masters of India's spiritual heritage found that the same virtues can be manifested in one's life time if the above Yuga producing movements could be enacted in the human body. Kriya Yoga had been designed on this pattern. In this design the Sahasrar, the main seat of the Spirit is taken as representing the body-sun, the mind as the moon and the Shushumna Nadi as the firmament containing the constellations of stars. By a technique of moving this 'moon' along Shushumna from the nearest point from the body-sun to the farthest point from the body-sun and back again along the same path a course of a lunar month can be enacted in the body. And to accomplish this takes only a fraction of a minute. Repeating this operation regularly at suitable time one can do the equivalent of a Kali Yuga, of a Dvapara, a Treta and of a Satya Yuga in a short period. By adopting superior techniques designed for the purpose it is possible to enact the equivalent of a Kalpa in one's very life time.

The most sensational observation of Swami Sri Yukteshvar was that the world now was in the Dvapar Yuga. He produced a long list of events and discoveries during the last couple of centuries showing that the human mind was gradually acquiring more and more capacities to comprehend finer and finer things in creation, to support his claims that the world was emerging into the higher Yuga of Dvapar from the Dark Kali Yuga during those periods. He predicted that human mind would acquire more and more knowledge in matters of electrical attributes and astounding discoveries in the field could be expected. He could not live to see how true were his predictions in this regard as proved by scientific talents in recent years. Human mind still was far away from comprehending capabilities of magnetic attributes, he said, which will be possible only with the advent of Treta Yuga.

For Yogis, however, it was a different matter; they could achieve all the 'virtues' associated with all the Yugas by enacting the process of Yuga manifesting technique in their Spiritual efforts in as short a period as a life time. Thus it would appear that the Hindu conceptions of Yugas and their application in spiritual culture is a feature of special importance.

5

Kriya

Kriya is the functional aspect, the potent technique, of the Kriya Yoga system. The technique has been designed on the pattern of the universal celestial movements of the solar system harmonising the same with physical and mental disciplines of Yoga. Although disciplines of many schools of Yoga may be termed as 'Kriya' it is the technique taught and handed down by Shri Shri Shyama Charan Lahiri Mahasaya of Varanashi that is universally known as Kriya. The word 'Kriya' actually means work. In order to make the purpose of such work conform to the intrinsic ideas of Karma of the Gita, Kriya technique has been designed on the pattern of the Hindi conception of the movement of the sun with its planets and satellites that cause unfoldment of inherent inner virtues associated with appearance and disappearance of the various Yugas.

In the chapter on the Yuga how the sun with its family of planets and satellites moves in a cyclic order in respect of the Grand Centre, the seat of the Universal Creative Force, causing unfoldment of the Yuga Virtues has been discussed. When the sun in the course of its movement comes closer to the Grand Centre, which is called the Vishnu Nabhi, the navel of Vishnu, the Lord of Lords of the Universe whence manifests the creator Brahma, inner virtues gradually manifest; and when the sun recedes away from the Grand Centre the virtues get gradually submerged. Manifestation of creation continues for a period of Kalpa of one thousand Daiva Yugas with the sun in this manner spinning all the while in relation to the Grand Centre. Other movements of the celestial bodies such as the moon and the earth continue concurrently with the cyclic movement of the solar system. While movements of the moon and the earth are easily comprehensible due to smaller length of time such movements consume, solar movement cannot be comprehended directly due to the vast expanse of time that has to pass for specific virtues of a Yuga to manifest.

It has been seen that in a period of a year of twelve solar months when the earth makes one complete revolution around the sun the moon makes a little more than twelve complete revolutions round the earth. In fact in a period of three complete solar years there are approximately thirty seven complete lunar revolutions round the earth. The period required by the moon to complete one revolution round the earth is known as a lunar month. Thus every three solar years may be taken as equivalent to thirty seven lunar months. Shastras have expressed age of a Yuga in terms of solar years, which can therefore be expressed in terms of lunar months as well. Thus the length of a Kali Yuga of twelve hundred years may be expressed as (1200/3 x 37) fourteen thousand and eight hundred months. This argument will be found important and very significant.

Spiritual leaders of India, from of old, considered that whatever there was in the Universe (Brahmanda) was also there in the 'pot' (Bhanda), the 'being'. The brain in the human body which is the seat of the Spirit is taken as the 'Sun'-principle in the body, while the human mind is considered as the 'Moon' principle. With these principles as the basis a technique has been evolved to move the moon-principle, the mind, between the nearest point to the sun-principle, the brain, by the force of breaths along Shushumna, which provides for the firmament, thereby enacting the movement of the external moon that constitutes lunar months. One such complete movement of the mind between the nearest point of the brain and the farthest along Shushumna is taken as the equivalent of a lunar month enacted within one's body itself. The Kriya Yogis call one such movement a 'Kriya'. To complete a Kriya, it can be easily appreciated, takes only a fraction of a minute. By repeating the Kriya one is able to accomplish the equivalent of the Yugas in a short time, within the span of one's lifetime. The Kriya Yogis affirm that finer virtues and capabilities that higher Yugas manifest in the course of thousands of years can be attained by performing the equivalent number of Kriyas. Higher techniques have also been designed in the system taught by Shyama Charan Lahiri Mahasaya by adopting which a Kriya performer is able to accomplish the fulfillment of Kriya Yoga even in as such a short period as six or seven years.

Another important feature is also involved in the technique of Kriya. In man Manas or mind and Prana, the aggregate of the five Raja or Kinetic principles that manifest in the Pancha Tattva, the Five Fundamental Principles, remain inter-tangled; the mind is the aggregate of the five positive or Sattva principles of the above Pancha Tattva; functions of Prana and Manas are various including the attributes of the organs of senses and of action. Expression of life lies in the stirrings of Prana; the mind also gets involved in the stirrings along with Prana as a result of the above condition. Consequence of performance of Kriya is gradual calming of the stirrings of Prana; and as Prana calms down the mind gets disentangled from it getting released from its restless state, a consummation to attain which all spiritual efforts are directed. In addition mental discipline woven into the practice of Kriya helps in drawing the tranquilled mind inward along the path of spiritual experiences and realisations.

In addition, with the controlling of the stirrings of Prana the involuntary nerves which otherwise continue to be active non-stop without rest also get rested thereby refreshing them. The voluntary nerves get their required rest when one sleeps or lies down; but not so the involuntary nerves which also should get rest if one aspires after long life. Practice of Kriya accomplishes this important aspect of living.

In an attempt to give a scientific explanation to the effects of Kriya, it is elaborated that the heart of a person throbs in order to draw in oxygen through breath for oxidising accumulated carbon inside due to metabolism processes. Deep breathing associated with Kriya or Pranayam that draw in more than normal oxygen within gives the heart respite for awhile and along with it the connected involuntary nerves. By this not only the heart gets a little rest but the mind is also released for awhile from the 'grip' of Prana.

The technique of Kriya is a marvelous method of controlling the difficult mind which perplexed even Arjun, the ideal Yoga aspirant of the Bhagavad Gita. Bewildered at the prospect Arjun submits to Sree Krishna:

> "Oh, Krishna, the mind is very difficult to control, it is very strong, rigid and maddening. I find it is as extremely difficult to control it as controlling the breaths."*

> *"Chanchalam Hi Mana Krishna Pramathi Valavad Dridham. Tasyaham Nigraham manye Vayoriva Su-duskaram." (Gita VI, 34)

Adoption of Kriya technique for spiritual pursuit, as such, is of immense benefit. Along with the controlling of the mind the Kriya Yogi is trained into delving deep and deep into the fundamentals of the scheme of creation and of life as established in the Upanishads and the philosophies of our spiritual culture.

For ages and ages Kriya had been the preserve of ascetics and saints who normally lived away from human society. The system was so highly esteemed and possibility of attainments by devotedly adopting it that the early masters thought only a very select and deserving few should be initiated into it lest the system was wrongly practised and applied for earthly gains or lest the price-less technique was in any way tampered with or misinterpreted. Many sound religious and spiritual teachings have been found to have been turned into unwelcome banal and vulgar features and decayed in the long history of India's spiritual efforts due to indiscriminate broadcasting of the teachings. The rigid attitude of the early Gurus of Kriya Yoga, even if it appears uncalled for and narrow today, saved the system from getting tarnished, debased and deviated from like many other valuable spiritual teachings.

The above barrier was, however, breached with the advent of Shyama Charan Lahiri on the scene, towards the middle of the last century, in 1861 to be specific. It was Lahiri Mahasaya's large-hearted kindness and unbounded loving consideration for his fellow worldly men and women that wrought the miracle. His ardent prayers to his Guru ultimately softened the Guru and 'the ice' was melted. He was allowed by his god-man Guru to initiate deserving and devoutly desiring persons, even a householder, into the secrets of Kriya. Thus it was Shyama Charan who became the fountain source of Kriya that spread gradually throughout the country and abroad. Kriya performers would always remember the ever-kind Lahiri Mahasaya for his munificence in this respect and worship his memory in their heart of hearts.

It is evident from the foregoing that Lahiri Mahasaya was not the propounder of Kriya Yoga. He had received it from his Guru the Holy Babaji Maharaj, who also must have received it from a Guru but nothing about whom is known. It has to be remembered that the Babaji Maharaj was well over three hundred years of age when Lahiri Mahasaya had met him. It was the year 1861 that provided the most important landmark in the history of propagation of Kriya Yoga in the country. Shyama Charan who was employed in the Civil Works section under Military department received official instructions to immediately proceed to Ranikhet, situated near the Himalayas in what is now the State of Uttar Pradesh of India. It was proved later that the official instruction to him was issued by mistake; another employee of the office was actually required to go. The mistake, however, was proved to be a boon in disguise of immeasurable value not only for Shyama Charan but for all human beings in futurity. During his stay at Ranikhet he unexpectedly and in strange circumstances met a Yogi saint who took him into his cave and divulged his identity; it was the Babaji Maharaj himself. He was told in the course of dialog that the mistake committed by his office in sending him to Ranikhet was not accidental; it was caused by the Yogic powers of the saint.

Babaji Maharaj was said to be his Guru in his previous birth as well. Shyama Charan recognised him as such after the holy Babaji had touched his body.

Suffice it to state that Shyama Charan was admitted into the secrets of Kriya Yoga by the Babaji Maharaj and he progressed rapidly into the higher stages while still in Ranikhet. Eventually the office detected the mistake and sent instructions to him to come back. By this time Shyama Charan had completely surrendered himself to the Guru and the ecstasies of Kriya Yoga. He made up his mind that he would never go back leaving the divine company of his worshipful Guru. But when he opened his heart to the Guru on the subject he was instructed otherwise. The Guru ordained that Shyama Charan must return and resume his erstwhile life of the householder; he was told that many important tasks were in store for him while in that life. At the beginning Shyama Charan protested and prayed to be allowed to pass the rest of life in the company of the Guru. Ultimately, however, he was persuaded to agree. In the process he successfully bargained for two concessions from the affectionate Guru. One was permission to initiate fellow householders also into Kriya Yoga to help them to achieve spiritual solace. The Babaji apparently agreed with reluctance but after imposing certain strict conditions. Thus when Shyama Charan returned to his old surroundings it was a different Shyama Charan; he was an accomplished Yogi and a profound Yoga Guru of the novel system of Kriya Yoga. Enlightened and accomplished disciples and grand disciples who had been duly authorised for the purpose spread the message and teachings of Kriya Yoga all over the country and abroad in later years. It may, however, be mentioned that minor differences are noticed in the system now being taught by different groups although the basic features still remain intact.

Kriya is intended to be a profound method of cleansing of the 'being' in its different phases of Shuddhi of different stages manifested in the course of its evolution, in order to get rid of the 'dross' that keep it shrouded from the Spirit. This cleansing or Shuddhi is a long drawn process and may be extended over several births. But to a devoted Yogi who performs Kriya with determined sustained and regular efforts complete success may be achieved during one's life time and even within a period as short as a decade. The Gita itself affirmed the difficulty involved in the pursuit. It says:

> "Of the thousands that labour for success hardly one does so with determination to succeed,
>
> Amongst thousands that perform with determination Hardly one knows Me in My essence."*

*"Manushyānām Sahasreshu Kaschit Yatati Siddhaye Yatatāmapi Siddhānām Kaschit Mām Vetti Tattvata."

It may seem from above that seeking success in Kriya, in spiritual efforts, is like wishing for the moon. That this is not so has been proved in the life of a number of Kriya Yogis. May be they had the benefit of 'cleansing' operations performed during their former births. However, due to kindness and compassion for fellow men and women in worldly life Sree Sree Lahiri Mahasaya had opened the door of secret Kriya Yoga to everyone who aspired after a divine life. Tradition established, under directions of the holy Babaji, is that Kriya has to be obtained directly from a Kriya Yoga Guru and to be handed down from the Guru to the initiate in a continuous chain. A Kriya Yogi can only act as a Kriya-Guru when allowed to do so under permission from his own Guru. Disciples of Lahiri Mahasaya used to be told to keep the teachings a closed secret and not to talk about it even with friends and relations who were not initiated into the secrets. So religiously this direction was followed that in cases even Kriya performers living as neighbours over twenty years did not know each other as members of the same spiritual fraternity.

Performance of Kriya entails several acts which evidently have been adapted from the Gita, the Yoga Sutras, Tantra Shastras and from conceptions on the Yugas. It has been recommended that Kriya has to be performed repeatedly assiduously, intelligently with one pointed attention, lovingly and continuously for long hours in a sustained manner to achieve tangible results.

Instructions contained in the sixth chapter of the Gita have been applied in the case of performing Kriya. In fact all the guidance laid down in this chapter of the holy book are found to have been incorporated for guidance of the Kriya Yogi. Principles with regard to selection of sites to establish the seat by the performer, the mode of sitting posture he has to undertake, attention he has to fix on and performance and end result of Pranayama very closely conform to the edicts contained in this chapter. In this case Kriya is but Pranayama with this difference that it has been regulated in the pattern of the course of the external moon round the earth and in relation to the Sun. The immediate end-result of Kriya is Pratyahara, as laid down in the Yoga Sutras, reversal of the direction of the senses from their objects towards the sensorium.

Initiation of a Kriya Yogi consists of a secret ceremony; it is an affair between the Guru and the initiate, but senior disciples may also be present. After teaching the initiate the different techniques and making him do them in his presence the Guru touching the body of the initiate excites in him, in between the eyebrows with eyes closed, the inner body-light variously termed as the 'third-eye', the spiritual eye or the Ajna Chakra. It appears as a bright sphere of white light with a deep blue central spot. The white aura is considered as Rādhā of the Kriya Yogis and the deep blue, almost dark, central spot as Sree Krishna, reflection of Kutastha Chaitanya in accordance with the spiritual interpretation of the Gita, discussed in the fore going. The initiate has to pay, under original instructions of the Babaji Maharaj five rupees to the Guru as Prayaschitta money, fees for spiritual ablusion of the initiate.

Performance of Kriya include the following:

* Mahā Mudrā
* Asana
* Kriya Proper
* Dhyāna
* Yoni Mudrā

Maha Mudra: This item evidently has been incorporated from Tantra Shastras like the Shiva Samhitā and Gheranda Samhitā. These Tantra Shastras contain elaborate descriptions about beneficial effects of Maha Mudra. The Mudra is a sort of physical effort to be performed by regulating the breaths. As an instant benefit performance of Maha Mudra invigorates the nerves, loosens the knee and ankle joints and refreshes the entire body outfit enabling the performer to sit on Asana in 'steady and comfortable' posture for long hours. Maha Mudra has to be done immediately before taking up Asana to perform Kriya. Some also advocate doing Maha Mudra before giving up Asana after completing Kriya, which relieves the performer of pains sustained during long period of keeping Asana.

Asana: Asana has been defined in the Yoga Sutras as a posture of sitting which imparts steadiness and comfort, while sitting.

"Sthira Sukham Asanam."

The posture referred to is undoubtedly related to seating to perform Yoga, spiritual efforts. Yogis designed various postures or Asanas for other purposes as well such as to cure certain bodily ailments or disablements. These latter have no connection with Yoga proper although they are generally described as Yogasanas. The various centres in the country and abroad engaged in teaching so-called Yogasanas are therefore not to be confounded with the principles and practice of the priceless and hoary inheritance of India in the realm of spiritual culture that is Yoga.

In all schools of Yoga sitting posture for performing Yoga technique advocated is the 'Lotus Posture' or Padmasana. This posture involves sitting with the legs interlocked, not only to aid in taking a steady and erect posture with the head, the neck and the body in a line but to help but to help in keeping the body remain seated when, with the achievement of Pratyahara, it tends to bend down or fall. To sit in this posture is uncomfortable to start with, the knees and the ankles giving intense pain. Maha Mudra performed before taking up Asana helps in reducing the intensity of the pain and retarding the start of such pain. However, with practice and beginning of the process of Pratyahara Padmasana becomes easier to sustain and comfort ensues.

Kriya: Kriya proper conforms generally to the definition of Pranayama as laid down in the Gita involving the secret technique of 'sacrificing' Prana, the outgoing breath, into Apana, the in-coming breath and vice-versa. The Kriya in addition lays stretch on the essentiality of attending to the three important Nadis in the body—The Shushumna, the Ida and the Pingala—and the different Chakras within the Shushumna. In the context of the pattern after which this profound technique had been designed, number of Kriya to be performed at each sitting is important. The Guru, however, is the proper guide who gives directions as to the number of Kriya to be practised at each sitting, and each day. The directions depend on the capabilities acquired by the adept and his determination and sincerity and attachment developed for the system.

It has been stated above that Kriya is a 'cleansing' operation, Shuddhi. It is an enactment of the lunar process which is in unison with the universal process of solar movement involved in the unfoldment of the fourfold Inner Virtues, the Chatuspad Dharma. It is said that in a solar year inner elements of the body such as flesh and blood get replenished. A solar year is the equivalent to a little more than twelve lunar months. Hence a Kriya initiate has to perform at least thirteen Kriya in one sitting to start with to ensure that the equivalent of a solar year has been accomplished. In fact, fourteen Kriyas are advocated, lest the first Kriya may be incorrectly done; such a course is called a Jada Shuddhi or cleansing of the physical dross. Number of Kriyas in a sitting has to be gradually increased to achieve to other finer 'cleansings' or Shuddhis, to decide which the Guru is the ultimate arbiter. Three solar years are said to constitute a part or a Khanda Yuga. Three solar years are equivalent to thirty seven lunar months; and performance of thirty seven Kriyas in a sitting is taken as equivalent to thirty seven revolutions of the moon round the earth, during which period cleansing of Nadis, finer attributes of the human body, are said to be achieved. Such an accomplishment is called a '*Nadi Shuddhi*'. A period of twelve solar years is taken as a Yuga which is four times a Khanda Yuga and hence equivalent to (4x37) one hundred forty eight lunar months. During this period the entire body apparatus gets re-charged and refreshed. Performance of one hundred forty eight Kriyas in one sitting is taken as enactment of this Yuga process thereby achieving 'cleansing' of the entire set of physical attributes of the 'being', the *Bhuta Shuddhi*.

A painstaking and determined Kriya Yogi is advised to complete at least three Bhuta Shuddhis each day. Some assiduous Kriya Yogis accomplish even four Bhuta Shuddhis a day. The most propitious hours are the dawn, the midday, the dusk and the midnight. These are termed critical hours in the day when the earth enters new phases after completing a quarter of its twenty four hour journey round its axis. Performing Kriya at such a juncture is considered extremely beneficial. It had been strongly advocated that at least three Bhuta Shuddhis should be completed each day—at dawn, midday and dusk—if midnight was considered inconvenient. By doing so one accomplishes three Bhuta Shuddhis a day, the equivalent of 'cleanliness' or unfoldment achievable in thirty six solar years in the normal way. Even allowing for lapse of a day or two due to physical handicap or domestic callings a Kriyavan can accomplish the equivalent of a Kali Yuga of twelve hundred years in the course of a little more than a month. Persevering in this way it is within the competence of the Kriya Yogi to complete the equivalent of a Daiva Yuga, mathematically speaking, in about a year's time. Accomplishing the equivalent of a Kalpa of one thousand Daiva Yugas, which is the aim and target of a Kriya Yogi within the span of one's lifetime, higher techniques of Kriya have been designed. It has been held by Kriya Yoga Gurus that a regular and devoted Kriya performer can reach the goal in about thirty six years. Cases have been known where success has been found to have been achieved in as short a period as six or seven years.

Basically the above is the technique of Kriya proper.

Higher techniques have been evolved to enhance the progress towards the goal of the Kriya performer.

Dhyana: After completing the required number of Kriya the performer has to sit quiet contemplating on the poise that results. Being absorbed in the poise is likened unto enjoying the nectar that floats up by churning the epical sea of milk. The mind has to be gradually detached from all thoughts whatsoever diving deep into the vastness of quietude and continued poise. This part is deemed essential to control the mind in order to plunge eventually into the 'nothingness' of Samadhi.

Yoni Mudra: Before giving up Asana the Kriya performer has to do Yoni Mudra. This is another feature of Tantric practices. Yoni means path, the path through which one is born. Performance of this sign, this Mudra, enables one to experience brilliant circular light within in between the eyebrows which is called the 'third eye'. It is the path through which one is born into spiritual sphere, hence the name. Subtle experiences are encountered within the 'third eye', this being the seat of Kutastha Chaitanya, the all embracing Spirit. Everything in creation may be revealed in the Kutastha. Shri Shri Lahiri Mahasaya used to term the Yoni Mudra as Jnana Yoga. However, with attainment of higher stages Yoni Mudra automatically manifests subtle and finer experiences by simply closing the eyes. Tantra Shastras are replete with eulogies about the benefits of doing Yoni Mudra sign.

Performance of Kriya or Pranayama constitutes Yajna, holy work; and enjoying the quietude and poise that results by performing the same is partaking of the 'remains', the Yajnasishta, as laid down in the Gita. Duration of sitting quiet and in poise can also be easily decided; performance of Kriya generates perspiration due to the heat that is generated in the body. This perspiration is not to be wiped off with any napkin or linen, but has to be dried up on its own. The performer is not to give up his Asana at least as long as the perspiration does not get dried up.

Higher Kriyas: The basic Kriya as stated above is known as the First Kriya.

Some say that Lahiri Mahasaya taught as many as one hundred and eight kinds of Kriya directed towards achieving powers and beatitudes laid down in all the Yoga Shastras. However, for attainment of Spiritual bliss and supreme elevation about half a dozen are deemed sufficient; of them the First, the Second, the Third and Fourth Kriyas have to be obtained from the Guru or in his absence from one who has excelled in these. The remainder can be divined out by the Kriya Yogi himself, as the principle underlying these are mastered after successfully completing the four Kriyas.

Perquisite for stepping into higher Kriyas is particular physical abilities, apart from acquiring penetration into 'inner' realisations. The physical ability lies in doing Khechari Mudra, another Tantra feature; it lies in the capacity to push the tongue through the septum behind the tonsil upwards. This is an essential perquisite without which higher Kriyas cannot be performed.

The Second Kriya is known as the Thokar Kriya, derived evidently from the 'Thokar' or jerk that has to be applied in the course of doing the Kriya. Mastering this Kriya gives one deeper penetration and finer and finer subtle experiences; experiencing 'inner light' and 'inner sound' become easy.

The Third Kriya is known as Omkar Kriya. This is derived from the fact that with diligent performance of this Kriya revelation of Omkar, the Pranava sound, becomes a reality. The nature and quality of this subtle inner sound have been aptly described in the first chapter of the Gita—as sounds of different battle conches of the Pandava heroes and of Shree Krishna. Revelation of the different strains of Pranava heralds attainment of different stages of concentration and Samadhi Thus the sound of the maddened black bees, the sound of Sahadev's conch Mani Pushpak; heralds achievement of Savitarka Samadhi or concentration with doubts. Audition of the note of the flute, Venu Dhvani, of Nakul's battle conch Sughosha, signals concentration dispelling any doubt but with circumspective analysis, which is Savichar Samadhi. Emanation of the gladdening note of the lute, figuratively said to be the sound of Arjuna's conch Deva Datta, indicates the concentration called Sananda Samadhi. Revelation of the continuous sound of the gong which is described as the sound of the great conch Paundra of Bhima, indicates that Sasmita or Samprajnata Samadhi has been reached. It is this sound that has been described in some Samhitas as the true Pranava sound. However, all the sounds described above are different strains of Pranava in its gradual course of revelation. The fearful sound of thunder and roar of the sea that is stated to be the sound of the Pandava king Yudhishthira's Ananta Vijay conch heralds attainment of true concentration or Asamprajnata Samadhi when all kinds of comprehension ceases. All the above five strains then mingling together can be heard as the bewitching sound of Lord Krishna's conch Panchajanya.

The first three stages of concentration or Samadhi are attainable in the course of performing the First and the Second Kriya also. The latter stages however, are attainable after mastering the Third Kriya. The Fourth Kriya is difficult to perform unless one has mastered the art of the Third. The Third and Fourth may be said to be extension of the Second Kriya. They cannot be performed, however, without being taught. Once the Fourth Kriya has been mastered the Kriya Yogi does not need any more guidance. He becomes a consummate Kriya Yogi himself. He divines processes of Fifth, Sixth and other higher Kriyas for himself in order to remain continuously immersed in the quietude and ecstasies. There may be quite a good number of Kriya performers who have been taught the Second Kriya; the number doing the Third is very low. The cases of performers of the Fourth Kriya is extremely rare, hardly a few. Swami Shri Yukteshvar had given the Fourth Kriya to only one disciple, and the latter had taught one or two more. Similar is the case with the other celebrated disciples of Shri Shri Lahiri Mahasaya.

With the gradual cleansing of the physico-mental apparatus the finer fundamental principles underlying creation can be realised. These realisations are associated with certain experiences.

Realisation of the Solid principle, Kshiti Tattva, is indicated when the out-going breath Prana flow through the middle nostrils without touching the sides and reaching up to a distance of nine inches down from the nose tip; a sweet taste is felt at the throat, and a desire to see yellow colour at the Kutastha; and a yellow quadrangular figure is perceived there-in. This experience may last for not more than twelve minutes.

The Liquid principle, Jala Tattva, is realised when an astringent taste is generated at the throat; a strong desire for white colour develops and a luminous half-moon shaped figure is perceived in the Kutastha; breaths flow down the nostrils up to a distance of twelve inches from the nose. The experience can last up to sixteen minutes.

Revelation of the Fire principle, Vahnni Tattva, is heralded by generation of a bitter taste at the throat, a desire to see red colour and perceiving a red triangular figure at the Kutastha. Breaths flow up to three inches within the nostrils. The experience may last for four minutes.

Air principle, Vayu Tattva, is realised when a sour taste is generated at the throat, longing for soury taste develops, attraction for blue colour develops and a blue circle is perceived at the Kutastha; breaths flow down touching the sides of the nose up to a distance of six inches from the nose. The experience lasts for a maximum period of eight minutes.

Akasha or Vyoma Tattva is revealed with generation of a pungent taste at the throat, longing for grey colour and perception of specks of variegated colour in the back ground of grey at the Kutastha. Breaths completely lose force and remain restricted within the nostrils. This experience can last for four minutes.

With realisation of the above subtle experiences the Kriya Yogi has to pursue the process towards fulfillment of the ultimate goal.

In the course of Kriya Yoga pursuit the Kriya Yogi attains to different spiritual heights. When he attains true concentration or complete Samadhi he is said to be in the Ajnān Chakra, the spiritual sphere of what may be termed "not-knowing." To the Kriya Yogis this is known as Paravastha of Kriya, the ecstatic stage to be reached after perfect performance. The next stage is rising up to the Vijnān Chakra, the sphere of subtle experiences. The highest elevation to attain is the Jnān Chakra, when the Yogi becomes "face to face" with the all pervasive spirit of Brahma—the Ultimate Creative Force, and becomes a "knower of Brahma", a Brahmavit. At this stage he becomes endowed with all Vibhutis and powers of a Master Yogi. Miracles become part and parcel of his being, being identified with the Brahma. The scriptural affirmation that "Brahmavit Bramaiva Bhavati", a knower of Brahma becomes Brahma-like, is fulfilled in such a life.

Manifestation of Pranava in the course of performing higher Kriyas constitutes stepping into the royal road to success. Pranava has been described in the Yoga Sutras as the "Expressor of God", "Ishvara Vachaka"; and as stated earlier, it has been compared to the "bow" for hitting the target and to the upper piece of fire-making pair of wood Arani, for making fire in the Upanishads. In the first case, the target is Brahma, and in the second case fire generated is for burning snares of bondage.

The Kriya Yogi endeavours to constantly remain immersed in the holy sound Pranava, the Omkara; and the deeper the concentration attained in this effort the quicker is he able to get over the attributes of senses and ultimately above the veil of Maya, Delusion. The different higher Kriyas have been designed to gradually attain the highest stage in this respect.

The different courses of Kriya techniques have been designed in such a manner that a Kriya Yogi proceeds towards perfection by passing through the stages of Dhyana (contemplation), Jnana (subtle experiences) Tyaga (renunciation) and Shanti (bliss)—the four steps in the progress towards ultimate success. Coming 'face to face' with Brahma at the Jnan Chakra, effulgence of Jnana flashes out. Lahiri Mahasaya termed it as Paravastha of Paravastha of Kriya, a stage beyond the Paravastha mentioned above. The Kriya Yogi is no longer required to physically perform any Kriya. He becomes engrossed in Jnana Yajna, the highest form of holy work advocated by the Gita. He is considered as enjoying 'pension' of Kriya. One can maintain his physical form as long as he wishes after attaining this supreme spiritual enlightenment. And when he decides that this mortal frame is no longer worth keeping he surrenders his self at the altar of the Supreme Spirit and gets completely merged and identified with Him. This consummation is attaining Kaivalya.

KRIYA
ITS PERSPECTIVE AND DISSEMINATION

Principles as well as technique of Kriya Yoga, as can be estimated from the foregoing discussions, have been based on the spiritual contents of the age old classical literatures. The most important scripture as far as the Kriya Yogi is concerned, however, is the Shrimad Bhagavad Gita, traditionally revered as the repository of the essential features of the Upanishadas and the Vedas. He has always been taught by all the Kriya Yoga teachers to treat this holy book as the main reference book. It is on record that Shri Shri Lahiri Mahasaya had got the texts of the Gita published and made a free distribution of the same to discerning readers. The Kriya Yogi fondly, reverentially and constantly keeps in his possession this scripture from the very time he gets initiated to Kriya up to the ultimate stage of fulfillment he might attain. Swami Sri Yukteshvar through his spiritual interpretations has shown how the tenets of the early philosophies such as the Samkhya and Patanjal lie ingrained in the back ground of the formulation of the messages of the Gita. While laying down essential features of spiritual endeavours this holy book has very clearly expounded some of the well known concepts of Hindu philosophies and spiritual messages which need to be emphasised. Without a clear idea of these concepts as laid down in the Gita it will be disadvantageous to make a proper estimate of the teachings of this profound holy book. Akshara, Svabhava, Brahma, Purusha and Karma and some of these concepts.

Akshara is the Indestructible, Imperishable, the Ultimate Supreme Spirit which is Param Purusha, Param Brahma and Param Atma—the only Real Substance that exists. Svabhava is Prakriti which provides for the Self in the presence of the Spirit and is thus called the Adyatma; while Karma is Shabda Brahma, Visarga, that cause evolution of ideas of 'beings'. To quote the relevant verse of the Gita:

> "Akshar is Param Brahma Svabhava is called Adhyatma Evolver of ideas of beings—Visarga is known as Karma"

> "Akshara Paramam Brahma Svabhavo Adhyatmamuchyate Bhutabhavoudbhavakaro Visarga Karma Samjnita." (Gita—viii,3)

From the above the fundamental and comprehensive principles of existence and creation as laid down in the message of the Gita can be traced. The Real Substance, the One without a second, is Param Brahma the Param Purusha. One of its aspects is Prakriti which provides for the 'creation' of Self, Atma.

Evolvement of this position forms the 'womb' in which the seeds of creation are cast, as elaborated in the following text:

> My vulva is the Mahat Brahma in which I cast impregnation, Thence it becomes possible for evolution of all beings."

> "Mama Yoni Mahat Brahma Tasmin Garbhanm Dadhamyaham Sambhava Sarvabhutanam Tato Bhavati Bharata." (Gita—xiv, 3)

According to Samkya tenets the first deformation that the Prakriti suffers under the impact of Spirit results in Mahat Tattva, which evidently is what has been termed as the Mahat Brahma above. Further transformation or deformation of the Prakriti is caused by manifestation of the Divine Sound Pranava that evolves at this stage. This Divine Sound is called the Karma or efforts bereft of all desires and attachments, the correct work advocated by the Gita. All the stages of deformation of Prakriti are due to impact of the Spirit and no stage is possible of 'becoming' without the presence of the Spirit. Thus the Spirit which does not in any way take part in the actual acts of transformation except being ever present remains inherent in every form that results, and the Spirit in such 'condition' is called Purusha, the Adhi Daivata of the created scene; while the Spirit that lies woven into all the forms created is called the Adhi Yajna which is synonymous with Lord Krishna the speaker of the Gita.

Again at another place the Gita explains the relationship or the link between Karma, Brahma, and Akshara.

> "Know that Karma evolves out of Brahma and Brahma from Akshara, Hence Brahma is all pervasive and constantly established in holy work."

> "Karma Brahmodbhavam Viddhi Brahma Akshara Samubhavam Tasmat Sarvagatam Brahma Nityam Yajna Pratishthitam." (Gita—iii, 15)

Thus Karma that has been defined above as Visarga, the Divine Sound of Pranava, that causes evolution of ideas 'beings' has been made the sheet anchor of spiritual efforts by the Yogis. This point has been elaborately described in the Kaivalya Darshanam, the Holy Science by Swami Sri Yukteshvar. The Kriya Yoga advocates that efforts are to be directed towards getting Pranava manifested and remaining immersed in the holy sound in order to attain Brahma for achieving complete emancipation, which is Kaivalya.

It has been emphasised that Brahma is also a created 'being' subject to the processes of appearing and disappearing in regular sequences like all other phenomena of various Yugas described as Aho Ratras. The secret laid down for reaching the supreme, the key for all created 'beings', is to link with the Chaitanya or Spirit that underlies all beings. To quote the relevant text:

> "Abrahmabhuvnallokah Punaravartinohrjuna Mamupetya Tu Kaunteya Punarjanma Na Vidyate" (Gita—viii 16)

> "All spheres beginning with Brahma appear and disappear again and again, But reaching Me, Oh son of Kunti, there can be no re-birth."

Kriya Yoga has designed techniques by adopting which one can gradually direct one's senses within by, in the process, getting Omkara manifested and then creeping towards the source of the Creative Force—Brahma and ultimately plunging into the Limitless and identified with the Param Atma.

Deformations of Prakriti and formation of different stages as a result thereof, according to the Gita, constitute the 'Field'—Kshetra and the 'knower' of this 'field' is the Spirit in every case. The 'knowing' of the 'field' and the 'knower' of the field has been defined as Jnana. The 'field' has been defined as:

> "The great elements, the Ego, the original Prakriti, the ten organs of the senses and action and the eleventh the mind, the five subtle objects, desire, aversion, happiness, sorrow, the mortal frame, consciousness and firmness— with all their ramifications constitute the Field in a nutshell."

> "Mahabhutanyahamkaro Buddhiravyaktamevacha Indriyana Dasaikancha Panchachendriyagochara" "Iccha Dveshah Sukham Duhkham Samghataschetana Dhriti Etat Kshetram Samasena Savikaramudahritam." (Gita—Xlll, 6 & 7)

The Gita describes the Knower of the Field thus while giving its definition of Jnana:

> "Know thou Me as the 'Knower' of the 'Field' in all fields, Oh son of Bharata, That which is knowing of the Field and of the 'Knower of the Field' is, I say, is Jnana."

> "Kshetrajnanchapi Mam Viddhi Sarvakshetreshu Bharata Kshetrakshetrajnyorjnanam Yat Tatjnanam Matam Mama." (Gita—Xlll, 3)

In line with the above edict of the Gita the Kriya Yoga teaches how to overcome the obstacles and rise up to the stage where Purusha and Prakriti 'perceive each other' face to face which flashes out as the dawn of Jnana. At this stage the Yogi goes above the bonds of creation and becomes like the Brahma. Further consecration at this pedestal ultimately leads to final emancipation—to Kaivalya.

The ancient Hindu savants in their boundless wisdom formulated well laid scriptures designed to emphasise how the above consummation could be successfully attained. A series of spiritual literatures collectively called Dialogue Between Krishna and Arjuna—Krishnarjun Samvad—may be mentioned in this connection. They are (i) Shrimad Bhagavad Gita, (ii) Anu Gita, (iii) Uttar Gita, (iv) Sapta Shloki Gita. The first of these has been exhaustively dealt with in this treatise; this is known as the Karma Yoga. The second which is a part of the Asvamedhik Parva of the Mahabharata has been described in the epic itself is but an elaboration of the Bhagavad Gita. The third, the Uttar Gita, forms a part of the Brahmanda Puran and is known as constituting Jnana Yoga. The last in the series is not a separate dialogue, but it is made up of only seven verses selected from different chapters of the Bhagavad Gita in which the principle of laying down of the Yogi's mortal frame so as not to suffer re-birth again has been laid down; it is known as the Laya Yoga.

Through the teachings contained in the above series of spiritual literatures, shown as dialogue between Lord Krishna and His famous friend and disciple Arjuna essences of the Vedas and the Upanishadas have been exquisitely expounded. Kriya Yoga by formulating different Kriyas has laid down potent paths for the gradual progress of the ardent and devoted Kriya Yogi to traverse all the stages and ultimately attain salvation from bondage of the illusion of births and rebirths.

After the door of the secrets of Kriya Yoga was first opened to the commoners through initiation of Shri Shri Shyama Charan Lahiri Mahasaya under mysterious circumstances, the process of dissemination of the secret teachings started first in trickles and ultimately through his successful and ordained disciples took the shape of a veritable country wide movement, under guidance of their Guru, as long as he was in his earthly life; and through their own enlightenment and organisational activities the famous disciples soon created a halo around the system of Yoga handed down by their illustrious Guru. Among the very prominent ones the names that come to the fore front are those of Acharya Panchanon Bhattacharya, Swami Keshavananda Paramhansa, Paramhansa Swami Pranavananda Giri, Acharya Ashutosh Shastri Mahasaya (Swami Kevalananda Paramhansa), Acharya Bhupendra Nath Sanyal, Acharya Brajalal Adhikary, Acharya Ram Dayal Majumder, and, of course, the most important and famous among them, Swami Sri Yukteshvar.

Acharya Panchanan Bhattacharya by initiating countless men and women in Kriya and by organising Arya Mission Institute in Calcutta and by publishing many Upanishads and other Hindu Shastras containing spiritual interpretations of Lahiri Mahasaya as heard direct from his mouth attracted attention of all spiritually thirsty people all over Bengal and elsewhere to the sublimity of Kriya Yoga. One of his disciples became a successful Kriya Yogi who was ordained to be a Kriya Yoga Guru by his own rights.

Swami Keshavananda Paramhansa who made Brindavan and Hrishikesh his spiritual homes established Katyayani temples in those holy places and by his high attainments attracted hosts of spiritually hungry souls from that part of the country to the fold of Kriya Yoga, many of whom became life long devotees of the system. He was one of the main attractions of the pilgrims that visited the above holy places.

Paramhansa Pranavananda Giri by his travels throughout Central and Northern India spread the supremacy of Kriya Yoga by his own example and precepts and captivated the imagination of the common people as well as of the elites of those regions including the Maharana of Udaipur and his family members. He had established Pranavashram at Varanashi for inculcation of the principles and practice of Kriya Yoga.

Acharya Bhupendra Nath Sanyal, who was an associate of the poet Ravindra Nath Tagore, established temples and Ashramas at Puri, Vindhyachal and several other places from where teachings of his Guru had been spread. He had several publications to his credit; the most monumental one was the Bhagavad Gita containing interpretations of the famous commentators in Hindu philosophy as well as spiritual commentaries of Shri Shri Lahiri Mahasaya.

Acharya Ram Dayal Mujumder was a recognized scholar in both oriental and occidental studies; apart from organising several social and educational projects all of which were directed towards diverting the attention of the educated to the priceless inheritance of spiritual learnings handed down through the ages he edited a monthly journal Utsav which was acclaimed as a gem in the field of spiritual literature. Through his efforts together with the efforts and influence established by his mentor Acharya Panchanan Bhattacharya Kriya Yoga penetrated its all-conquering influence among the hard core classical and traditional scholars in and around Calcutta and other parts of Bengal.

Acharya Ashotosh Shastri Mahasaya (Swami Kevalananda Paramhansa) was an unassuming saint. But unostentatiously he with his captivating and ennobling influence penetrated into many spiritual and organisational activities of his more famous contemporaries. Countless men and women came to his feet for solace and spiritual enlightenment. His association with the organisational activities of Paramhansa Yogananda in India contributed immensely in making the Ranchi Brahmacharya Vidyalaya a pioneering institution in the country.

Acharya Brajalal Adhikary like Acharya Ashutosh Shastri Mahasaya was of unassuming demeanour. His attainments as a Kriya Yogi was, however, unparalleled.

He also had initiated countless men and women into the solemnities of Kriya Yoga. One of his celebrated disciples was late Bahadur Singh Singhee of Singhee Park, Calcutta.

Swami Sri Yukteshvar had been the foremost among his illustrious co-disciples who continued with the liberalising process that started in 1861 at the holy meet at Ranikhet. He had organised broad-based organisations for propagating the solemn fundamental teachings of the esoteric Shastras of Hindu culture. Among his hundreds of Kriya Yoga disciples were not only the educated from urban societies but from innumerable humble folks of distant villages in the districts of Midnapore, Howrah, and Hooghly of Bengal. His Yogoda Sat-Sanga Sabha devoted to inculcate aspects of life which were considered healthy both in the ancient Hindu systems as well as in the Western systems were taken to the distant villages as well. It is significant that many among his rural disciples had become very advanced Kriya Yogis. His crusade against perpetuation of wrong ideas with regard to correct readings of the Hindu almanacs and of his convictions with regard to interpretations of the concepts of various Yugas was amazing. It is through his various writings that one finds what may be said to be the philosophy of Kriya. His organising the saints and savants in classical learnings into an All India Organisation, the Sadhu Mandal, with his Holiness the Sankaracharya of Gobardhan Pith, Puri as the General President with an executive named the Sadhu Sabha of which he himself was made the working President—the Sadhu Sabhapati—speaks eloquently of his organising capacities.

The most significant and startling part of his effulgent life was his meeting with the Holy Babaji Maharaj at the Kumbha Mela, held at Allahabad in 1894. As a sequel to this mysterious meet Swami Sri Yukteshvar had written his famous book The Kaivalya Darshanam The Holy Science, which may be said to be the fore-runner of the sojourn of India's priceless inheritance, the Kriya Yoga, to the west over the seven seas.

KRIYA YOGA
GOES TO
AMERICA & THE WEST

Paramhansa Yogananda proved to be the chosen vehicle to carry the age-old inheritance of India of Kriya to America. He was the second famous monk from India to the New World. The first was the ever famous Swami Vivekananda whose sweeping exploits in that part of the world earned him the epithet 'Hurricane Monk of India.'

In the year 1920 a Conference of World's Fellowship of Faiths was held in Boston, United States of America which Yogananda had attended as a delegate from India. From that year up to the time of his demise Yogananda lived in America devoting practically whole of his life in propagating Yoga in that country except for about a short period of a year when he came to pay a visit to the country of his birth.

Born in an affluent family of Yogi parents Yogananda's was a rare birth; both his father and mother were Yoga disciples of Shri Shri Lahiri Mahasaya, and thus he had a natural claim to be the representative to carry the message of Kriya Yoga to the west. When he was a mere baby he was placed on the lap of Lahiri Mahasaya by his parents, and the great Yoga Guru made a significant comment; "this lad will become an engine in his future life", the Yogiraj had remarked. From his very childhood Yogananda, then Mukunda Lal, showed great attraction for religious men and monks. An unknown sooth-sayer who had visited his house during this period had warned the inmates that the boy would in future relinquish the comforts of family life and would become a mendicant. All these were no doubt advance signals of what was in store for him in the future.

Mukunda Lal lost his dear mother when still very young. This heart-breaking bereavement coupled with his in-born aversion for worldly life strengthened his determination to become a monk. He was quietly on the lookout for a spiritual guide. His secret searchings, however, brought him no success, but he continued with his endeavours. Meantime he pursued his studies and eventually passed the Matriculation and Intermediate Examinations of the Calcutta University. He was now a grown up young man full of physical and mental vigour. He decided that his hour of destiny had arrived. One day without telling anybody he fled home and went straight to Varanashi. Reaching that holy place he was perplexed as he knew no place where he could go. When aimlessly wandering, fortunately he caught the attention of a saint, Swami Jnanananda Paramhansa, Head of the famous Bharat Dharma Mahamandal, who was surprised to see a handsome lad of immature age clad in saffron clothes moving about anxiously. Perceiving that the young man did not realise what type of a life he had chosen to lead the Swami took him to his Ashram. There he advised the young man that the life of a Sannyasi was very hard and difficult and that one had to undergo studies in the Shastras for preparing himself for such a life. The kind Swami affectionately asked Mukundalal to stay in his Ashram and take up studies of the Vedas. Mukundalal readily agreed.

Shortly afterwards while one day Mukundalal was going his way in the city and was passing through the crossing of that road with another his eyes fell on a saintly person who was coming towards the crossing along the other road. The saint's glowing countenance captivated Mukundalal. But as he did not know him Mukundalal passed on and soon was out of sight of the saint. Strangely Mukundalal soon felt that he could not proceed any further, his mind was filled with the charming appearance of the saint; he felt that his feet had been practically immobilised. He turned back and walked toward the road crossing in quick pace. To his utter surprise he saw that the saint was standing on the very spot where Mukundalal had seen him first and looking towards the direction of his path. As if under a spell Makundalal ran to the saint and fell on his feet in complete surrender. The saint affectionately raised him in his arms and exclaimed, "Thou hast come at last my boy." The saint was none other than Swami Sri Yukteshvar; and the miraculous meeting meant that Mukundalal had got the Guru he had been yearning for all these years. Swami Sri Yukteshvar took Mukundalal to his residence at Rana Mahal, Varanashi and by close questionings learnt that his new find was a son of his co-disciple Bhagavati Charan Ghosh of Calcutta and that the boy had fled home in search of a Guru and to become a full fledged Sannyasi. Mukundalal was initiated by the Guru into Kriya Yoga at Rana Mahal and was advised by the Guru to prosecute his studies after returning home to prepare himself to become a great Sannyasi. He should at least obtain the University degree, he was told, as great tasks were in store for him in the near future. Mukundalal was very reluctant to start with as he strongly desired to become a Sannyasi then and there. However, by patient reasonings Sri Yukteshvarji was able ultimately to persuade him to agree. The first foundation for the possibility of Kriya Yoga to pass on to America was laid by this strange meeting between the two, in fulfillment of the unexpressed wishes of the Holy Babaji Maharaj.

Mukundalal returned home to the great relief of his anxious father and other members of his family. He also agreed to take up his studies, but not in any Calcutta College. He would like to get admitted to the College at Serampore. His unexpressed desire, of course, was to be very near his loving and worshipful Guru who was a resident of Serampore. This had to be conceded to and Mukundalal achieved what he dearly wished for. But he showed little considerations for studies; his entire time was passed in company of the Guru. When the time for final degree examination arrived Mukundalal found that he was totally unprepared and suggested that he would sit for the Degree Examination the following year after making proper preparations. But the Guru would have none of it; his stern orders were that he would sit for Examination that very year. Mukundalal was left with no alternative and reluctantly had to do whatever he could to make himself ready for the final ordeal. Meantime he received instructions from the Guru to follow certain procedures which Mukundalal followed. He, however, realised it was a hopeless task. But he had to carry out the orders of the Guru. When the final results were published Mukundalal was beyond himself in joy and pleasant surprise; he had come out successful and had obtained the degree. But he publicly ascribed, throughout his life, that his success in the Degree Examination was solely due to his Guru's miraculous powers. The year was 1915.

Now that he had fulfilled the condition Mukundalal could not wait any longer; he was ordained by Swami Sri Yukteshvar as a Sannyasi of the Shankara order with the new name of Swami Yogananda. He carried this name during the life time of the Guru. After the Guru's demise and after his return to America from his year's sojourn to India he assumed the new name of Paramhansa Yogananda.

Yogananda cherished high ambition for doing something great in life. In fact Swami Sri Yukteshvar infused this desire and determination in him from the very moment the two had met. Like most of his kind in those days Swami Vivekananda's exploits were his ideals. In 1916 Yogananda went to Japan. But he did not stay there for more than a week. The then atmosphere in that land was not to his liking. He returned home by the next available steamship. The only tangible gain during this sojourn was his meeting Capt. Rashid on the ship in the return journey. The two became so much attached that Capt. Rashid took Kriya from Yogananda on the ship. The friendship fruited into a relationship of co-operation and collaboration when Yogananda was finding it difficult to make headway in his missionary activities in America. Capt. Rashid joined him as the Organising Secretary and by adopting American methods of publicity firmly established Yogananda's reputation and influence as a Yoga teacher.

In 1917 Yogananda started a Brahmacharya Vidyalaya with the blessing of his Guru and under the patronage of Maharaja Manindra Chandra Nundy of Cossimbazar. This Vidyalaya was ultimately shifted to Ranchi where its work and function earned wide publicity and fame throughout the country as an ideal institution for education of boys. One Sunday afternoon in 1920 while Yoganandaji was the Principal of this institution he saw a vision, standing at the door of the kitchen store of the Vidyalaya, that he was lecturing before a large gathering of Western audience both men and women. At once the Swami exclaimed that he was going to America. So saying he rushed to his apartment and made preparations to leave for Calcutta by the evening train. The inmates who by this time came to know about this development rushed to his apartment to find that their dear Acharya, their Principal, was ready to start for the Railway station. Those who knew him from his early years, his life long associates, realised that a man of vision that he was all his life he would certainly go to America.

Coming to Calcutta he started moving about as a man inspired and driven by some unknown force. By tireless efforts he succeeded in procuring a delegate's ticket to the forth coming World Fellowship of Faiths Conference to be held in Boston and with financial assistance offered by his father he booked a berth in the ship that was soon to sail for America. In the excitement of quick moving sequences he even forgot to meet his Guru and obtain his approval and blessings, the Guru that groomed him all these years for this eventuality. The Guru, however, did not fail his dear spiritual child. He kept detailed information of the Chela's various movements in silent interest and expectations. On the day the ship was due to leave the shores of the port of Calcutta Swami Sri Yukteshvar was seen scaling up the ladder of the ship, standing by the wharf; he obtained a pass through the good offices of another disciple to embark on the ship. As soon as Yogananda saw his Guru coming up on the ship he ran in all reverence and gratitude on to his feet. He was bitten by remorse in failing to remember his Guru all these days but was at the same time overjoyed at the thought that his loving Guru did not fail him at this crucial juncture. Sri Yukteshvar, as was his wont, did not have time for sentiments and for minor failures. Immediately he led Yogananda into his cabin and the two were closeted inside for some time. Eventually the Guru gave the disciple last minute instructions about his mission. It is said that the Guru handed to him a copy of the Kaivalya Darshanam, the Holy Science which was printed that year and advised him to base his preachings and teaching along the line indicated in this book. A discerning critic of the activities and preachings of Swami Yogananda in America and other countries of the West would find that Yogananda did never depart from the basic principles laid down in this wonderful book.

Although Yogananda used to boast when he was in India that he would never adopt any change in his routine and behaviour, he proved by his actions that he was a master artist in adopting changes that was found more suitable. To give an example, Yogananda kept beard, moustache and flowing locks of hair and as a Sannyasi, wore saffron clothes. When embarking the ship many friends advised him to at least shave off his beard and moustaches. But he brushed aside these friendly advices saying that he would never forsake bearings of the Sannyasi that he had been. But soon friends received a letter from him written from the port of Aden that he had a clean shave of his beard and moustache at that port. Later he revealed to his co-passengers who were mostly Europeans tried to avoid his company mainly for his 'uncouth' facial hairs. The same proneness to change was also noticed in his missionary activities.

To begin with Yogananda persevered with an attitude of ascetic stoicism in whatever he did both in his personal living as well as in his missionary activities. As a Sannyasi he had the least consideration for money; he did not charge any gate fees for any body intending to attend his lectures nor did he indulge in costly ads and publicity. The result was that response of the American public was extremely poor. A lecture that could be heard free was considered cheap and not worth bothering about; and poorly publicity was hardly noticed. The situation came to such a pass that he could not make money enough for his keep. It was natural therefore that he had to depend on remittances from home, from his father, for about two years, for his expenses. It was at this juncture that Capt. Rashid joined him. He immediately jumped into American methods displaying attractive posters, costly ads and heavy gate money for attending the Swami's lectures. All inhibitions smacking of stoicism were cast aside. And success soon followed.

In his methods of initiation into Kriya also Swami Yogananda added innovations. Perceiving that the average American found it difficult to sit in lotus posture, he taught that he could sit erect on a straight-back armless chair, legs hanging, and practise Kriya; initiation was also a mass affair; instead of direct contact between the teacher and the taught—the Guru and the novice—the whole affair was reduced to something like an indoor class. Another startling innovation was that Second or the Third Kriya was allowed to be practised without having to do Khechari Mudra. All these innovations or rather deviation from the regular methods could not find favour with devotees and lovers of Kriya Yoga.

It is pertinent to note that an American intellectual Dr. Wendel Thomas, an American professor,—in his book 'Hinduism Invades America' (New York 1930) while eulogising the broadness of outlook of Swami Yogananda and comparing him as the best among all the Hindu Missionaries that ever came to America, pinpointing adoption of American methods by him remarked, "He has plunged headlong into American life…. who knows if the message itself is not changed in the long run."

Did the message change as the learned professor had apprehended? Evidently the answer is 'no'. By and large Kriya appeared to have grown firm roots in that country. Some American disciples certainly experienced sublimities of Kriya such as perceiving inner 'light'—Jyoti—and manifestation of Omkara. Mr. Lynn, variously called by Yogananda as Saint Lynn and Rajashi Janakananda— the latter after Lynn was made a formal monk—may be cited as an example. During his stay in India in 1935/36 the author acted as the Swami's private secretary; and in that capacity had access to many correspondences. One day when the author was sitting beside Swamiji a bunch of mail arrived. From amongst the lot Yoganandaji picked one envelope address on which was written in hand. He quickly tore the envelope, lovingly went through the hand written letter. At one stage he jumped up in joy and exclaimed, "This chap was surely an Indian Yogi in his previous birth." Swamiji then showed the author the relevant lines in the letter that moved him emotionally. The line read, "my pen stops everything has become light ****". Lynn wrote the letter with so much devotion and concentration that he raised himself to subtle spiritual experiences.

A mysterious experience brought Lynn to Yogananda's folds. Once Swami Yogananda fell into acute financial stringencies. When he came to know about the precarious conditions his heart ached. He did not wish for any affluence that was bestowed on him by Providence; then why was he being harassed. He went to a secluded place and started praying and lamenting as to why he had been entangled into such fetters. While in his deep prayers he heard an inner voice assuring him that he had nothing to fear. He came back to his Head Quarters completely poised and reassured. In a few days time he had a pleasant surprise; he received a handsome donation from an unknown individual by post and all financial worries were over for at least the time being. The sender of the generous donation was one Mr. Lynn from another city of America. On the other side Mr. Lynn who was then in some domestic trouble one night had a strange dream. He saw an Indian Yogi asking him to remit some substantial donation to Swami Yogananda at his Head Quarters at Mount Washington Centre at Los Angeles. Lynn considered his strange dream the following day and decided to send a good donation to Swami Yogananda. Along with remittance Lynn wrote that he would visit the Swami on a specified day. On the allotted day as Lynn entered the Temple hall in the ashram and his eyes fell upon the bust of Lahiri Mahasaya placed at a suitable niche on the pulpit he exclaimed in utter dismay, "This was the Yogi I had seen in my dream." Lynn was initiated into Kriya by Yogananda that very day; and from that very day Lynn began long and devoted practice of Kriya. Whenever he would find time during his busy hours—he was one of the most renowned man in the Insurance world of America—he would go into his practising Kriya. After the demise of Swami Yogananda Lynn, then Rajashi Janakananda, became president of Swamiji's organisations in America and India under the Swami's own will.

Another devoted disciple is Daya Mata, one time Swamiji's secretary and at present President of his organisations. She is an intelligent and lovable personality and a Kriya initiate of long standing. Her devotion to Kriya and her loyalty to Swami Yogananda and his line of Gurus is remarkable. It was her great credit and a proof of her devotion when she successfully persuaded the then Sankaracharya of Gobardhan Math, Puri to ordain her as a female monk of the Sankara Order. There were many more celebrated men and women in that country who embraced Swami Yogananda's teachings.

Swami used to declare that the teachings he had brought from India were of Universal application irrespective of faiths and cults; and that the technique he taught, which he named Yogoda, was the best art of living capable of imparting harmonious development of body, mind and soul. He also developed a system of free hand physical exercise which he called Yogoda exercise based on the principle of contraction and relaxation. This was advocated to be practised before starting performance of Kriya every time. It was claimed that this exercise loosened different joints of the body and invigorated the body outfit. His position as a high spiritual teacher was well established within a few years, and the success he had achieved in his missionary activities was phenomenal. While the Head Quarters of his organisation was located on its own expansive property at Mt. Washington, Los Angeles many more branch centres were also established in various cities of the United States. Some were also established in some parts of South America.

When Yogananda realised after Capt. Rashid had joined him that a poorly looking man could not expect social recognition in that affluent country he gradually turned himself into an affluent person, with the rapid success he had achieved. In fact he was considered a millionaire in contemporary America, and he attracted notice of many citizens in the higher echelons of American society. He was the first Indian to have been permitted an audience with the then president of America, President Coolidge, in the White Hall as a token of recognition of eminence he had acquired.

In his spiritual teachings Yogananda advocated performance of Yoni Mudra, which he preferred to call Jyoti Mudra, by which a devotee could experience Jyoti and hear Omkar sound after continued and prolonged efforts. Considering the hurdles involved in performing different Kriyas properly this method was found by him to be more suitable. Moreover this was found to be in keeping with the precepts contained in the Sadhana, Procedure, chapter of the Holy Science of Swami Sri Yukteshvar. Yoganandaji revealed to some of his close associates like the author that it was through consistent and deep involvement in the manifestation of Pranava that he had attained success in his own spiritual illumination.

However, Swami Yogananda passed away in 1952 leaving behind a well established and sprawling chain of organisations in America and India and thousands of loyal and devoted followers all over the world. There was no doubt that he had made a lasting imprint of Yoga learning and teachings in American life.

When the course of dissemination of Kriya Yoga is considered in its wider perspective three important land marks are prominently discernable. The first was the mysterious meeting that took place in 1861 at Ranikhet at the foot of the Himalayas between the Holy Babaji Maharaj and Lahiri Mahasaya; the second was, again a surprise and mysterious meeting at the Kumbha Mela at Allahabad in 1894, between the Holy Babaji and Swami Sri Yukteshvar; the third land mark was the meeting between Sri Yukteshvar and his spiritual child Mukundalal, the future Swami Yogananda in the early part of the second decade of the present century at Varanashi. The liberalising process in the dissemination of Kriya Yoga that had ensued at the holy meet at Ranikhet thus culminated in the spread of the essence of this profound spiritual system over to America.

It is up to the present devotees of Kriya Yoga, specially those in America for whom Swami Yogananda had devoted all his cares and love, to keep up the tradition in its true essence and purity. What would appear to a sympathetic observer from a distant land is that more emphasis should be laid on the intellectual and theoretical aspect of the system instead of cherishing a loving and devoted memory of the illustrious one so as to be able to comprehend the inner depths and wider perspectives the hoary system offers. Propagation and scrutiny of the principles and techniques of Kriya Yoga both in America as well as India would dispel blind craze for the supernatural and for the so called god-men. Kriya Yoga system is an inheritance of utmost value and possibilities which should properly be made more and more public for the good of mankind.

MAHAMUNI BABAJI MAHARAJ

The Holy Babaji Maharaj has been an enigma. The worshipful Guru of Shri Shri Shyama Charan Lahiri Mahasaya, he was the fountain source of dissemination of the system of Kriya Yoga to the world in modern times. He was not known by any name, and perhaps appropriately. He remains for ever the most revered original Guru of the Kriya Yogis. In a hymn composed by Acharya Swami Satyananda Giri Maharaj the Babaji had been mentioned as Mahamuni Babaji, the great sage. Considering the concepts cherished by Kriya Yogis this was perhaps very fittingly applied. The author chose to maintain this epithet in attempting to write something about this Holy of the holies. Swami Sri Yukteshvar who had the great fortune of having met the mysterious saint at least twice used to mention that the very name Babaji was so holy that when his name was uttered even once his entire being would appear to have been totally purified. To the Yogiraj and his advanced disciples the Babaji was much more than the God.

It pains a worshipful heart when it is perceived in the present days that even much humbler individuals are making a bee line at Ranikhet and some even claim to have had received benedictions from this superman. Gullibility of men knows no limit. Some of the illumined disciples of Lahiri Mahasaya claimed to have had darshan of this holy saint; Swami Sri Yukteshvar, Swami Keshavananda, Paramhansa Pranavananda, Acharya Panchanan Bhattacharya have claimed to have had darshan of Babaji Maharaj. One of the biographers of Lahiri Mahasaya, a grandson of the Yogiraj, tried to belittle these claims as untrue. His endeavors, however, are found to be an attempt to paint Lahiri Mahasaya as their family property forgetting that the great Yogi was a world teacher. None of the Yogiraj's progenies could claim to have attained higher stages in Kriya. Such opinions as against versions of the Yogiraj's several saint disciples can be contemptuously ignored.

No authentic account is available about the Babaji's name. Some writers pointed out that among contemporary sages in Northern India Babaji was also known as Traimvak Baba and Shiv Maharaj. But there is no parallel confirmation of this from the accounts that can be had from the closest saint disciples of Lahiri Mahasaya, nor any reference to this effect in Lahiri Mahasay's recorded talks. It is preferable therefore not to accept such assumptions. A picture is also now seen, claiming it to be of the Babaji, professedly drawn from visions of some eminent men in the line. But from accounts available directly from those who had avowed having seen this unusual god-man do not fit in the features found in the pictures.

It may be recalled that from among the disciples of Lahiri Mahasaya at least four famous ones had claimed to have personally seen the Babaji Maharaj. They were Swami Sri Yukteshvar, Paramhansa Pranavananda Giri, Paramhansa Keshavananda and Acharya Panchanan Bhattacharya. While no information is available about the opinions of the latter two saint disciples as to what the Guru of their Guru looked like, Swami Sri Yukteshvar gave out specific descriptions.

One day, sometime in the year 1932, Swami Sri Yukteshvar paid a surprise visit to the dormitory where this author was living as a college student. After passing some time the saint asked the author to accompany him to the ancestral house of Paramhansa Yogananda, which was not far from the dormitory. We were not required to go to the house as Shri Sananda Lal Ghosh, third brother of Yoganandaji, appeared on the road in front of the house. Sananda Lal is a reputed artist, expert in drawing portraits. He is now in his eighties and is still hale and hearty. Seeing him the Swami said he was looking for him. Then he asked him to draw a picture of the Babaji Maharaj stating that this would not be difficult for him. He was simply to make the picture of Lahiri Mahasaya in a standing position, make locks of hair a little longer and flowing over the shoulders, free end of the narrow Dhoti worn made to go round the shoulders and resting on the right arm held in a right angle like that of an up-country cow boy, and the left hand hanging parallel to the body. Face would be exactly like that of Lahiri Mahasaya but should look much younger. The Swami assured Sananda Lal that he could do it without much difficulty. But the artist became bewildered. How could he paint such a picture he demurred and whose picture he would succeed in drawing he would not know. He expressed strong diffidence in succeeding to accomplishing the task as desired. Sri Yukteshvar re-assured him of his success and left. However, Sananda Lal did not dare to handle the task, perhaps considering the holiness of the individual involved. From the description given a clear idea as to how the holy one had looked like, at least as far as how Sri Yukteshvar had seen, can be made out.

Paramhansa Pranavananda Giri Maharaj gave an account of description of the Babaji as he had seen him in the company of his own Guru Lahiri Mahasaya as also of some talk he had had with the holy one. The account was published in the edition of the Gita which was named after him—the Pranava Gita—by his disciple Sri Jnanendra Kumar Mukherji who is now over one hundred years of age and is still hale and hearty. As Pranavananda was talking to his Guru in the latter's sitting room Lahiri Mahasaya suddenly got up in a hurry and excitement, walked up on to the courtyard and Pranavananda followed him, and fell prostrate on the feet of an up-country looking young man. Pranavananda was dismayed at his elderly Guru showing such veneration to an unknown youngster. Getting up Lahiri Mahasaya directed Pranavananda to show his veneration to his Guru Babaji Maharaj. Pranavananda immediately did as asked, but wondered how the Babaji could look so young. The three had dined together and during their talks Pranavananda asked the holy one a few questions. The following is an account, briefly, of the questions and answers.

Q: How old was Babaji?

Ans: Normal life span of man was 120 years, but one could lengthen the life span by performing Kaya Kalpa, the technique of re-juvenation. He had done three such Kaya Kalpas and was in the latter half of the fourth.

Q: How long would the Babaji remain in his present body?

Ans: He would like to continue in his present form for sometime more as he had some more important task to accomplish.

Acharya Bhupendra Nath Sanyal, one of the youngest among the direct disciples of Lahiri Mahasaya, had not personally seen the Babaji Maharaj, but he had ideas about how his Param Guru looked like. One day during Swami Yogananda's sojourn to India in 1935/36 the author accompanied him when he went to meet the Acharya. The Acharya was then in Calcutta on a short visit and was putting up with one of his disciples, late Dr. Arun Mukherji, in his house situated behind the Bethune College, North Calcutta. Yoganandaji at that time was engaged in collecting materials to write a book on the saints of the country. His main interest in this meeting was to elicit information about Babaji Maharaj, knowing that the Acharya was a direct and advanced disciple of Lahiri Mahasaya. When asked if the Acharya had seen the Babaji and how he looked like the Acharya smilingly replied that he had heard that those who were very advanced in Kriya became similar in appearance—like Lahiri Mahasaya. Asked if he had heard if the Babaji was still living the Acharya replied that he had heard of one looking exactly like Lahiri Mahasaya living in the Northern region of Siberia.

Countless followers of Kriya Yoga firmly believe that the Holy Babaji is still alive and guiding the spiritual life of the people of the world. That he was alive up to the fourth decade of this century there is ample evidence.

In 1942 two friends of the author, Late Nalini Mohan Majumdar, younger brother of Acharya Swami Satyananda and Sri Tinkari de of 54/1 Malanga Lane, Calcutta went to witness the Kumbha Mela then being held at Hardvar. There they searched out Swami Keshavananda Paramhansa and revealed their identity that they were also Kriya performers. The Paramhansa entertained them with endearment and wished them happiness. In the course of discussion Tinkari asked the saint if by then Babaji Maharaj had arrived at the Kumbha. The saint replied that on previous occasions he had the privilege of Babaji's Darshan by such time, but this time he had not yet met him.

Late Kumud Datta and his wife, of Sambhu Nath Pandit Street, South Calcutta, were Kriya disciples of Acharya Swami Satyananda. They had a cousin, a handsome young man, who was the only son of his parents. The young man was employed in a bank and was newly married. One day as soon as he reached his office in the morning he received a telephone message from home that his wife had an accident and that he should quickly go home. The young man rushed home to find that his dear wife was already dead. She had a fall while scaling the stairs of the house badly injuring the back of her head. He was greatly mortified and lost all urges to live. When in such a disturbed frame of mind one day he visited the Dattas. He said he would search for a Guru. The Dattas possessed a copy of a special issue of the 'Inner Culture' published from the Head quarters of Swami Yogananda's organisations in America. This issue displayed attractive pictures of many of the disciple saints of Lahiri Mahasaya. As he scanned through the pictures he pointed to a portrait of Swami Sri Yukteshvar and said he would go to him and take him as his Guru. The Dattas told him that he was unlucky and that the Swami was no more. He then pointed to the picture of Paramhansa Keshavananda and learning that the saint was still alive decided that this saint must be made his Guru. He asked the Dattas where he could find the whereabouts of the saint. The Dattas referred him to this author who was then holding some executive position in Swami Yogananda's ashram centre in Calcutta. One evening when the author was engaged in some errands a young man came in and introduced himself. When told that the person he was speaking to was the very man he was looking for he came and embracing the author requested for a letter of introduction to Paramhamsa Keshavananda, narrating in the process his tale of sorrow. The author said he was moved, but not knowing the saint personally he would be of no help. This much was known that he might be available in either of the two Ashramas, Katyayani temples at Brindavan or Hrishikesh. The only person whose introduction would carry weight would be Late Ananda Mohan Lahiri, one of the grandsons of Lahiri Mahasaya who was then living in Ranchi. The young man then requested for a letter to Ananda Mohan to enable him to procure the required letter of introduction. The author did and armed with it he immediately went straight to the Howrah Railway station to catch the train that would leave for Ranchi shortly.

The latter part of his story was narrated by the young man himself after his successful endeavour. He said that he went to the Katyayani temple at Brindavan first but learnt that the saint was at Hrishikesh. This was the first time the young man had ever gone outside Calcutta. But he was not deterred. He got into the next available train to Hardvar and from there to Hrishikesh. After some searchings he found out the place and entered the Ashrama. It was a little before dusk, he found many people squatting on a spread out mattress on the floor facing a saintly looking person with matted hair and beard seated on a raised chair. He soon recognised the saint as the man of his destiny. He took up seat at the back of the rows and listened to the discourses, but agitated within. Would the saint listen to his prayers and accept him as a disciple? he was musing. After all those present had left one by one and he was alone face to face with the saint he gathered courage, rose up and fell on the saint's feet. Getting up with folded hands he narrated his cause of sorrow and prayed to be accepted as a Kriya disciple. The saint said he had been refusing to give Kriya to anybody because nobody practiced Kriya seriously after receiving the same. Pointing to many of his ascetic disciples living in his Ashram the saint remarked that all were fallen Yogis, Bhrashta Yogis, as no one practiced Kriya as extensively as advised. The young man was heart broken at this refusal; he mused for a while and then touching the saint's feet he prayed for his blessings and his grace in his determination to receive Kriya; he would proceed to the jungles of Ranikhet in a last attempt to meet Babaji

Maharaj, no matter if he was devoured by predatory animals like tigers in the attempt. He then got up and turned to go off. At this time he overheard the saint murmuring, "in the end he will have to come to me"; the saint then called him back and said that he would initiate him the following morning. At this sudden change in his good luck the young man's joys knew no bounds.

The following morning he was duly initiated to the secrets of Kriya Yoga which assuaged his mental torments. After a few days' stay at the Ashram the young man returned home; and at the earliest opportunity he met the author. His entire countenance was beaming with joy when he narrated his arduous experience.

The above accounts are intended to show that up to that year at least the Babaji was supposed to be alive, as passed on by one of the saint disciples of Lahiri Mahasaya who was known to have had personal Darshan of the Holy of the Holies. The Kriyavans implicitly believe that the Guru of the Gurus is still guiding their spiritual life from his high spiritual elevation.

As to the picture of Babaji Maharaj, no one currently in circulation is authentic. One was drawn by Sananda Lal on outlines given by his illustrious brother Paramhamsa Yogananda. Yogananda claimed to have seen Babaji in a vision. But this picture does not conform to the descriptions given by Swami Sri Yukteshvar. Saint Kriya Yogis rarely bothered about any concrete picture of the persons they worshipped as gods; they cherished their memory and their teachings in the pure sanctuary of their hearts. An American admirer of Swami Premananda, a disciple of Yogananda who is engaged in Missionary activities in America for about half a century with permanent centre in Washington D. C., painted a picture supposed to be that of Babaji Maharaj as seen by him in a vision. It was a large portrait but was no where near the descriptions as obtained from Swami Sri Yukteshvar.

Devotees of Kriya Yoga should have veneration enough not to be swayed by unauthenticated accounts of the Baba emanating from time to time, some time intentionally spread by gullible people. One gentleman wrote an article stating that he had met the Babaji running an Ashram at Brindavan. Poor soul! How could he imagine that such a lofty saint would be found enmeshed in such worldly affairs as having to run an Ashram or a monastery? The Mahamuni Babaji does not belong to any age or clime; his is an universal personality, guiding the destiny of mankind all the world over to its Divine birth-right. Unlimited salutations to the holy one.

Bibliography

- Shrimad Bhagavad Gita—Adhyatmiki Vyakhya—By Swami Sri Yukteshvar Giri

- Shrimad Bhagavad Gita—By Swami Jagadishvarananda

- Shrimad Bhagavad Gita—By Dr. Bhagvan Das & Annie Besant

- Shrimad Bhagavad Gita—By Matilal Roy

- Kapilashrameeya Patanjal Yogadarshan—By Samkhyacharya Shrimad Hariharananda Aranya

- Kaivalya Darshanam, The Holy Science—By Sadhu Sabhapati Swami Sri Yukteshvar Giri

- Hinduism Invades America—By Wendel Thomas (New York, 1930)

- Life of Saint Issa—By Nicholas Notovich (New York, 1890)

- Yogiraj Shri Shri Shyama Charan Lahiri—By Swami Satyananda Giri

- Yogiraj Shri Shri Shyama Charan Lahiri—By Abhoy Charan Lahiri

- Shrimad Swami Sri Yukteshvar Giri—By Swami Satyananda Giri

- Pranav Gita—By Paramhansa Swami Pranavananda Giri

- Sapta Shloki Pranav Gita—Jnanendra Mukhopadhyay

- Manu Smriti

"Dadu"

Acharya Sri Sailendra Bejoy Dasgupta
(1910–1984)

Exalted direct disciple of Swami Sriyukteshvar Giriji Maharaj

Dadu,
We are your children surrendered at your feet.
Thank you for guiding us with your light.
Please accept our quiet offering.

About the Author

The Author is a direct disciple of Swami Sri Yukteshvar. He also came in intimate contact with several other direct disciples of Yogiraj Shyama Charan Lahiri. He was a student of the Ranchi Brahmacharya Vidyalaya established by Paramhansa Yogananda.

Titles available from Yoga Niketan:

The Scriptural Commentaries of Yogiraj Sri Sri Shyama Lahiri Mahasaya:
Volume 1

The Scriptural Commentaries of Yogiraj Sri Sri Shyama Lahiri Mahasaya:
Volume 2

Srimad Bhagavad Gita: Spiritual Commentaries by Yogiraj Sri Sri Shyama
Charan Lahiri Mahasay and Swami Sriyukteshvar Giri

A Collection of Biographies of 4 Kriya Yoga Gurus

by Swami Satyananda Giri

Kriya Yoga

by Sri Sailendra Bejoy Dasgupta

Paramhansa Swami Yogananda: Life-portrait and Reminiscences

by Sri Sailendra Bejoy Dasgupta

Yoni Tantra: Commentary on Selected Verses In Light of Kriya Yoga

by n.w. "kashi" ("bala gopee")

LaVergne, TN USA
02 December 2009
165749LV00006B/14/P